About The Authors

Bret Oldham

Bret Oldham is the author of the acclaimed Amazon Best Seller, *Children of the Greys*, and the follow up book, *The Baby Takers*. Bret has made several national television appearances in the United States, Canada, France, and Bulgaria including shows on Bio, Discovery, CBC Canada, History Channel, TV7 Bulgaria, and RMC Decouverte in France. He is a frequent guest on Internet TV and radio shows around the world and has been interviewed by numerous online magazines and newspapers. Bret has been a contributor to several books by other authors and online magazines. As a featured speaker, he has presented for numerous paranormal and UFO groups, organizations, and conferences across the United States.

Contact info – haloproductions@live.com

AFTERLIFE ENCOUNTERS

Ghosts, Spirits, and Near Death Experiences

Julie McVey-Oldham

Bret Oldham

Edited by **Julie McVey-Oldham**

Cover art by **Jeffrey Oldham**
Copyright © 2019 Jeffrey Oldham
www.oldhamart.com

Published by
House Of Halo
Foley, AL. U.S.A.

ISBN: 978-0-9891031-7-6

Julie McVey Oldham

Julie McVey Oldham has been interested in the paranormal and UFOs for many years and has spent the last 25 years researching and studying the phenomena. She has a professional background in psychology and counseling as has worked with many different populations. Julie has a BA in psychology and Master's degrees in Marriage and Family Counseling and Religious Education. Julie is a truth seeker and has found that her study of psychology has opened her mind to explore other areas of thought and consciousness. She has practiced yoga and meditation for many years, and in 2017, she completed her yoga teacher training and currently teaches yoga and barre.

Table of Contents

Acknowledgements

To Jeffrey Oldham, Thank you for your valuable help and creative collaboration with this book cover. We appreciate you more than you know.

To all those who contributed to this book, Your stories are incredible. You provided us with a wealth of knowledge to help us all learn more about the afterlife. You opened up and shared your very personal experiences which will give all the readers of this book comfort in knowing that consciousness lives on after death. Your stories taught us that the bond of love is forever and that we have no reason to fear making the transition to the other side. Our sincere thanks to each and every one of you for making this book possible.

FOREWORD

Most people will not publicly reveal a belief in ghosts. The stigma of being labeled delusional or crazy for espousing such a belief remains a strong deterrent. Yet, accounts of such visitations have been told for thousands of years. Experiencing a paranormal event is often what changes a person's belief in the spirit world. This type of event can conjure up deeply rooted fear. Is it our own innate fear of death and what lies beyond that keeps us from searching for answers? Perhaps, it is the fear that what we have been taught by religion may be wrong. Maybe, it is nothing more than a natural fear of the unknown. Hollywood has done its part in cashing in on these long-held emotions pertaining to the spirit world. Almost every film even remotely related to the genre is released for the purpose of scaring the audience. This only serves to heighten our fear of the afterlife. Sadly, in recent years, the film industry has amped up this fear. Now, much of the paranormal is attributed to some sort of demon, which, in the real world, is not true.

The surge of "reality" ghost hunting shows has not helped much in this regard. These shows often play up the demonic theme. Often, they are filled with bad acting and an overemphasis on dark entities as a cause for the possible haunting. While dark entities have and do wreak havoc in people's lives, most hauntings are far from anything wishing to inflict harm on the living. Yes, it can be frightening to witness objects moving on their own. It is also frightening to see misty forms, shadow people, or full body apparitions. This fear of the unknown activates the fight or flight response, which causes most individuals to run away. In actuality, most paranormal activity is caused by a lost soul trying to get our attention. How this is manifested is determined by how much energy the ghost or lost soul has. There is a difference between a "ghost" and a "spirit." It is our belief that ghosts are lost souls who have become trapped in a middle dimension. There can be various reasons for this entrapment. An individual may be convinced that he will go to Hell, if he fully crosses to the other side. Others may be trapped because of strong attachments to people, places, and things in this world. Eventually, the lost soul realizes he is trapped. The phenomenon, created by this soul, is a plea to the living for help; it is this plea for help that is often misidentified as a haunting.

Spirits, on the other hand, are souls who have fully crossed over to the other side and who choose to return for short durations of time. This can be to warn a loved one or to comfort a loved one. They may assure their loved one that they are happy and okay on the other side. Sometimes, they return to, simply, visit. They may make their presence known in ways that only the loved one would recognize, and they may speak or appear. Often our deceased loved ones will come to us in dreams relaying messages or re-living special memories with the living. Most people find great comfort in any of these methods. One thing we can learn from either ghosts or spirits is that there is no death. It is only transition. We are all made up of energy, and energy cannot be destroyed. It only changes form when we shed our earthly bodies. Another aspect that needs to be mentioned is residual haunting. These are not intelligent hauntings but rather energy imprints that replay over and over. Imagine a scene in a movie that gets stuck and loops the same few seconds of a scene repeatedly; this is similar to a residual haunting. These hauntings are usually triggered by strong emotions associated with a particular event. The event could be a wedding, funeral, birth, battle, etc. So much energy is released during this event that it, somehow, leaves an imprint in time, which surfaces in our dimension.

The stories in this book are true accounts of visitation from and to the other side of the veil, each with its own details and reasons for taking place. While some of these experiences were understandably frightening, most were comforting to the person that witnessed and experienced them. The encounters also frequently changed the subject's own view of death. Nothing, however, has a more profound effect on one's belief and perception of death than having a near death experience (NDE). Almost unanimously, the individuals interviewed in this book expressed that their fear of death had dissipated after experiencing an NDE. Many became less religious but more spiritual with a strengthened belief in God, a Supreme Being, or Source. NDE experiencers encountered both ethereal beings and sometimes other spirits. They recognized their earthly bodies, and most did not want to return, except for the strong sense of unfinished business. One of the most fascinating and important aspects of those who have had a near death experience was the description of feeling the most intense, unconditional love that they have ever felt, which was often accompanied by an extreme sense of sereneness and peace. It is our hope that, after reading these incredible real life, true stories, you will have a better understanding of what happens when we die and experience less fear regarding death and the afterlife. We all know that no one gets out alive. The good news is that's okay.

Chapter 1

Spirit Contact and Communication

Many people believe that, when our physical body dies, our souls go to a place called Heaven or Hell. Heaven is believed to be a beautiful and peaceful place, whereas Hell is described as a torturous lake of fire and eternal damnation. Where we end up depends on what kind of life we lived during our time on earth. This concept of reward or punishment in the afterlife has been the foundation of most of the major religions of the world for centuries. However, it is a man-made construct; it is not congruent with the experiences of countless people who have had first hand encounters with the afterlife in various ways. To these individuals, death of the body is not the end. What happens to our soul essence after death is not as simple as religion teaches us to believe. In the following chapters of this book, you will read incredible accounts of various encounters with the afterlife. Some are sightings of full body apparitions; some received amazing messages of love, guidance and protection from loved ones who have crossed over. Still others, actually crossed the threshold between this life and the next and came back to tell their stories. No matter what method of contact or communication was used, the result was always the same. The experience changed the person's perceptions and feelings about death.

Belief in some sort of afterlife is nothing new. Since pre-historic times, humans have maintained the belief that an individual lives on in a non-physical form after death of the body. Throughout the course of the evolution of homo-sapiens, many great civilizations believed in life after death. The Romans, Greeks, Chinese, Celts, Egyptians, East Indians, and most of the indigenous tribes of the Americas and Africa all shared some type of belief in the afterlife and demonstrated those beliefs in various religious practices and rituals. In ancient times, being able to communicate with the spirit world was often held in high regard. Such was the case with the various priests, shamans, medicine men, and mystics from these cultures.

Much has changed since those ancient times regarding our beliefs about contacting the spirit world and what awaits us on the other side of the veil when we die. Now, many people believe that attempting to contact the dead is sinful or that one is practicing some type of witchcraft, even Satanism, by doing so. Nothing could be further from the truth. Even with these rampant misguided beliefs, there are still countless individuals out there every day trying to contact those on the other side. It was the Spiritualism movement that began in the 1840's that brought the practice of contacting the spirit world to the mainstream masses. Spiritualists believed that those who had crossed over into the spirit world had both the desire and the ability to communicate with the living. It turned out that this principle was, is, and has been true since ancient times.

It was the Spiritualism movement that first brought about the use of psychic mediums who were believed to be individuals with the unique psychic ability that enabled them to communicate with spirits. Although controversial, mediums are now quite common and also popular. So strong is the desire to communicate with deceased loved ones through medium ship that some mediums have become very famous and have charged exorbitant fees to their clients. Mediums all work in their own way and will often use different methods to contact the other side. Séance's (the ritual of a group of people gathered around holding hands in a circle to receive spirit messages) were quite common at one time. Usually a medium would conduct the séance. Some mediums claim to do "channeling," which is where the medium allows the spirit to take control of his body and speak through him using the physical voice. Other mediums will hold objects from the deceased to make contact. Through holding the object, they may receive images in their mind's eye or simply hear the spirit speaking directly to them. Many people, who have used mediums, have found comfort in the process and have been pleased with the results of a psychic session.

Another popular form of spirit communication used by the general public is what is known as the Ouija Board. I am sure most everyone is familiar with the Ouija Board. Most have probably used one at some point in their life. The Ouija Board is flat and rectangle shaped. It is made of either pressed cardboard or wood and has the alphabet, numbers, and the words yes, no, and good-bye printed on it. A small, heart shaped, usually plastic planchette is used by the participants by placing the tips of their fingers on it as it moves around the board, supposedly guided by spirits answering questions presented by the users. "Planchette writing" has been used for centuries to contact the spirit world. However, it was not until World War One that the original Ouija Board began to be used for that purpose.

As you will see in the following chapters of this book, those who now reside in the dimension of the spirit world often have as much desire to speak with us as we do with them. So much so, that it is often the spirits making the first contact, as was the case in many of the accounts in this book. The spirits will use whatever means available in order to do so. Some spirits have a stronger energy, and that makes communication with us easier. Other spirits will draw energy from whatever source they can find, including us. Both spirits and ghosts have been known to materialize into full body apparitions, often appearing as solid as you and I. Some are even able to speak while in this solid form. Other forms are also taken by those on the other side in order to make themselves known to the living. These include human shaped shadow forms in black or sometimes white misty ectoplasm with no particular shape. Sometimes they will appear as balls of light and move erratically through a room. They will also move objects, turn lights on or off, and bang on doors and walls. These are all forms of spirit communication. It takes a lot of energy and effort for a ghost or spirit to execute any of these things, and they should not be ignored.

There is a reason for a ghost or spirit to go to such lengths to make their presence known. Imagine the sadness and frustration you would feel, if you were in the spirit world and doing your best to garner someone's attention only to be ignored or, worse yet, feared. It is up to the living to determine the meaning behind these types of incidents. Are they being done by a ghost that has had their space invaded and simply wants to remain in solitude? If so, the ghost may try to scare away the living. Is it a trapped spirit searching for help from anyone who will listen? Are they the spirits of relatives or friends who have returned to deliver important messages or warnings to their earthbound loved ones? As you will see in the stories in this book, not everything one experiences in the paranormal is dark and evil—far from it.

The advancement of technology has made it easier than ever to speak to the other side. Hand held digital recorders are now frequently used to record EVPs (electronic voice phenomena) by picking up and recording voices which are outside the hertz level of human hearing capabilities. Modern computer software audio programs have become very useful in analyzing the digital recordings in order to pick out, clean up, and better hear voices of the spirits/ghosts speaking. Often, warnings and messages are delivered this way. Many times EVP work will aid in determining who is at a location, why they are there, and what they need or want. The field of spirit communication and paranormal research has grown exponentially with the use of these modern recording devices and computer software programs.

One of the most controversial methods of modern spirit communication is in the area of Instrumental Trans Communication or "ITC" for short. This is specifically spirit communication through the use of electronic equipment. This could include such electronic devices as cell phones, televisions, and radio. The premise of ITC is not all that new. Two of the world's most famous scientists were early pioneers of ITC work. These two scientists are Nikola Tesla and Thomas Edison. As early as the 1920's, Thomas Edison was working on a device he called the "Telephone to the Dead" and even reported it to *Scientific American Magazine*. Unfortunately, he did not complete the project before he died. It did not matter though because, like so many other inventions, the great Nikola Tesla had already beaten him to it. Tesla did it through radio waves. For years, it was thought that Guglielmo Marconi was the inventor of radio, but in the 1940's, his patent was taken away and given to its rightful owner, Nikola Tesla, whose work Marconi had stolen. Tesla's patent still stands today, and he is now considered the inventor of radio. It was through these first radio waves that Tesla began to hear voices speaking, sometimes in languages other than English. He believed these voices to be the voices of the dead. What we do know for sure is that he was not picking up radio stations. If not from radio stations, then where were the voices coming from?

Many years would pass before Tesla's claims, that spirits could use electronic devices to communicate with the living, would take hold. Although there were a few attempts to record EVPs by others over the years, it was not until 1959 when Swedish film producer Friedrich Jurgenson inadvertently caught voices while recording bird sounds for a film he was producing. While playing back his recording, he happened to notice that he had also recorded people talking even though there were no other people around. These voices that he recorded were not just random people. He recognized them as his deceased father and his deceased wife. In fact, his deceased wife was calling him by name. He was so taken by the experience that he subsequently began to purposely try to record more voices; he eventually contacted his dead mother who left him a message. Eventually, he wrote a book about electronic voice phenomena and is considered to be the godfather of EVP. In 1964, Jurgenson's book on EVPs garnered the attention of Latvian psychologist, Dr. Konstantin Raudive, who contacted him with his interest in the subject. That interest blossomed, and in 1965, they began working together doing ITC experiments based on Tesla's premise that spirits could communicate with us through radio waves. During the course of their work together, the pair recorded over 100,000 examples of EVPs though Instrumental Trans Communication using a radio set to an empty frequency.

Interest in ITC waned until around 2002 to 2003 when paranormal hobbyists began to modify regular am/fm radios in order to use them to contact spirits. They did this by simply disengaging the scan button, which enabled the user to speak to the ghosts and spirits and then listen for response in the white noise of radio waves. Eventually, ghost hunting television shows started using them and the moniker "ghost box" or "spirit box" was coined. They have since become a very popular, albeit controversial, method of spirit communication. Skeptics claim that what is being heard during a ghost box session is merely fragments of actual radio stations coming though. While it is true that small snippets of radio shows will come though during the scan, that in and of itself, does not explain the vast amount of evidence to the contrary. Experienced users, who are serious about ITC work, will record and analyze the audio from a ghost box session. They learn to discern the different tone and sound of an actual radio station from those of a spirit speaking. When the scan mechanism is disengaged, it does not stop or hesitate on a radio station that is picked up. It quickly passes by them thus making it impossible to hear a full sentence; one may hear just a few quick words or bits of music. I have conducted many spirit box sessions over the years. Many times, I have heard and recorded full sentences that were direct responses to something that was asked or said. How could a radio station do that? It cannot, nor can it say your name or names of other people participating in the ghost box session, which I have heard countless times. I have recorded further proof that the spirits use electronic devices to communicate with us. I, and others, have heard cussing coming through the radio. These were words that were clear and words that are certainly not allowed by the FCC on the airwaves without being fined a hefty sum.

Skeptics also claim that what is being heard through a ghost box is merely "audio pareidolia," which is hearing words or sounds that are not there, but our brains will go to a word that is familiar to us in order to process it. While this can happen in some cases, it does not explain how people recognize the voice of a friend or loved one speaking to them during a session. Nor does it explain the very personal details that are often said by the spirits. I have recorded audio that I later cleaned up and analyzed that revealed these types of personal and sometimes embarrassing details about someone who was at the session. When I would later reveal these things, that I would have no way of knowing other than from the spirit box, they would corroborate that it was true. I have asked things to the spirits about the past that they would know. I have asked things about the present in which they answered correctly. I even did an experiment with friends one night where we made cue cards that contained obscure words. We held them up and asked them to read them, which they correctly did. In another experiment, a friend of mine, who lived two hours away, and I both turned on our ghost boxes at a pre-designated time. I wrote a phrase down. I then asked the spirits to tell my friend through his box what the phrase was. My friend did the same on his end. Neither of us knew what the other had written down. One of us caught the full phrase, and the other was able to catch one word of the phrase. We both considered the experiment to be a huge success. At other times, warnings about the future were delivered to loved ones, which, when ignored and not taken seriously, happened. These various experiments, sessions, and messages with ITC showed me that those who have transitioned to the other side see the past, present and future. The space–time continuum as we know it does not exist in the realm of the spirits.

Ghosts, who have become trapped in our plane of existence, or spirits, who have crossed over, have been communicating with the living since the dawn of mankind. They always have and will use whatever mode and method necessary to do so. Modern technology has made it easier for us and, perhaps, even easier for them as well. Communication from the spirit realms is negated only by the unwillingness or fear to listen. It may not be what we are taught by society or religion, but you will see various types of spirit communication through the numerous, very personal afterlife encounters in this book. Those that do listen are rewarded beyond measure, and their lives and beliefs are forever changed in a positive and meaningful way.

CHAPTER 2

Grandma's Last Goodbye

Chandra always had a wonderful relationship with her grandmother. She cherished the moments they spent together. When Chandra gave birth to her first child, a boy, her grandmother was filled with pride and joy. Mama Martin, as the family affectionately called her, enjoyed playing with her new great-grandson Connor and spent as much time with him as possible. Time, however, was something that was fleeting for her. On August 5, 2009, Mama Martin had a heart attack and passed away. Connor and Mama Martin had a strong attachment to each other. On the night she died, Connor woke Chandra and her husband; he was crying inconsolably. They could not figure out what was wrong with him, or why he was so upset. Suddenly, Connor stopped crying. A few minutes later, they got a call from Chandra's Dad telling her that her grandmother had just passed. It appeared that she had died around the same time that Connor stopped crying. It was as if he knew that she was about to pass. When she died, it was as though he felt the same peace that Mama Martin did. Connor was only two years old at the time, and Mama Martin never got the chance to tell her sweet little great-grandson goodbye. Her biggest fear was that Connor would not remember her. Sometimes, unfinished business can keep souls earthbound. In other cases, spirits simply want to let loved ones know that they are okay. Their love may be so strong that they cannot move on and find peace until they say goodbye in their own way. Such was the case for Chandra and little Connor.

It had been approximately two months since her grandmother had died. Chandra was sitting in the den watching television. She had stayed up with

Connor, hoping that he would soon get tired and fall asleep. Her husband had already fallen asleep on the couch. Finally, Connor fell asleep and then so did Chandra. In the middle of the night, she heard a voice that woke her. "I'm gonna get ya, get ya, get ya," the voice was saying. She opened her eyes and could not believe what she was seeing. It was her grandma, Mama Martin! Connor was awake, and Mama Martin was playing with him. She was sitting at the end of the couch where Chandra's husband was sleeping. Connor was busy bringing toys to Mama Martin and then taking them back. Mama Martin had her hands positioned in a clapping motion. She continued to say, "I'll get ya, get ya, get ya." Chandra sat there awe struck by what she was witnessing. She had just awakened and was not fully prepared for what was happening right before her eyes.

She looked right at her grandmother and said, "Mama Martin?" Mama Martin replied by telling Chandra to go back to sleep. She would watch Connor. Mama Martin looked to be about the same age as when she died, only healthier. She was wearing one of her favorite outfits rather than the clothes of her burial. Chandra's first thought was to run upstairs and grab the video camera to record the event. She changed her mind for fear that her grandmother would disappear, while she was retrieving the camera. She decided to just take it all in and enjoy the moment. Mama Martin kept insisting that Chandra go back to sleep, but, of course, Chandra was too excited to do that. Instead, she decided to ask Mama Martin some questions. "Mama Martin, you know you're dead right?" Mama Martin told Chandra that she knew she was dead. As they continued to chat, Mama Martin continued to display her sense of humor. As she sat by Chandra's, still sleeping, husband, she joked about how he could sleep through anything.

Eventually, little Connor got tired and crawled back up on the couch and went to sleep. Chandra got up and opened the front door. She could see that the sun was beginning to rise. Chandra knew that it would soon be time to wake her step-children for school. She began to worry about how she was going to explain Mama Martin's appearance from the dead, for she appeared as solid as a living person. Mama Martin got up and started to walk towards the door. Perhaps, she sensed Chandra's apprehension about explaining her appearance to the other children. Maybe, she did not want to scare them. Chandra asked her where she was going. Mama Martin answered in a very matter of fact way, "You of all people know where I'm going." Chandra knew what her grandmother meant. Mama Martin had been very religious and frequently read and studied the Bible. This was another reason Chandra was surprised to see her grandmother's spirit; she was not one of those people you would expect to return from the grave. Chandra asked her grandmother where her walker was. Mama Martin told her that where she was going she did not need it anymore. When Chandra asked her how she was going to get there, Mama Martin simply replied, "I walk." As she exited the door, Chandra got up to follow her. As Chandra stepped outside, the sun was coming up over the horizon. A bright ray of sunlight blinded Chandra. When she regained her sight, Mama Martin was gone.

Chandra's emotions were running wild, as she tried to come to terms with what had transpired. She could not lie down or get any rest the entire day. The excitement of Mama Martin's visit was something that she could not wait to share with others. Unfortunately, her account of her grandmother's return from the other side did not receive the response that Chandra anticipated. With the exception of her mother and father, most told Chandra that she had been visited by a demon. Some even went so far as to proclaim that it was the devil himself that had come to Chandra. Chandra vehemently denied their conclusions. She insisted that no demon or the devil would have told her the things that her grandmother did. During the course of her conversation that night, Mama Martin had told Chandra to study the Bible and attend church regularly; someday they would see each other again. That other worldly advice from her grandmother had a profound effect on Chandra. Soon after the incident, she began to read and study the Bible on a regular basis. She also included her husband and children in these studies.

Mama Martin's return from the dead was not Chandra's last encounter with the afterlife. A few years ago, she was in the midst of running errands when she had another other worldly encounter. On that particular day, she made her first stop at the post office. As she was walked across the parking lot, she heard someone call her name. She looked around and spotted a middle age gentleman approaching her. Chandra was friends with this gentleman and his elderly father. They exchanged greetings and made small talk. Chandra asked him about his dad. "We're not talking," the man replied. Chandra was very surprised to hear this. She knew that this man and his dad had always been very close. The man explained that he and his father had had a bad fight a couple of weeks prior and had not spoken since. Chandra told him how sorry she was to hear that. The man then said, "If you see my dad, please tell him I love him, and I'm sorry for the argument. Tell him it's not his fault." Chandra assured him that she would do this but thought that he would see his dad long before she did. At that point, she turned and continued to walk into the post office. She assumed the man was following her, but when she looked back, he was gone. She figured he had gotten into a vehicle. Since the post office was very busy, she must have lost him in the commotion.

A couple of weeks later, Chandra happened to run into his dad, and they began chatting. During the course of their conversation, Chandra mentioned that she had talked to his son recently. She told him that his son had mentioned their fight. She went on to relate that his son had expressed how sorry he was and that he loved his dad. "Are you sure?" The dad asked with a hint of shock in his voice. "Oh yeah," Chandra replied. "Well he's dead," the dad sadly proclaimed. Those words shook Chandra to the core. She told him that she might be mistaken about the date, even though she knew that was not the case. She did not want to upset the elderly man with the idea that his son had returned from the grave with a message, albeit an important one. The gentleman then told Chandra that he and his son had been in a bad argument on the day that his son passed away. During the argument, his son suffered a massive heart attack and died. He had done CPR but could not save his son. Chandra decided to relay the message from the son in the best way possible. She told the elderly man that she was sure his son had forgiven him and again reiterated that it was not his fault. Looking back on the event now, Chandra feels that the deceased man chose to appear to her because he knew she would deliver his message. That is exactly what she did. Chandra helped that spirit finish his unfinished business. Chandra's act of kindness helped both the father and the son to find peace.

Chandra will never forget her encounters with the afterlife. She has told her son Connor many wonderful stories about the great grandmother that loved him so much. Over the years, Mama Martin has made her presence known to other family members too. In 2015, it was Chandra's mother, Joan, who was contacted. This time, however, she came in a more subtle way, a dream. This was not just a normal dream about a deceased relative. This one was much more important, and it seemed that Mama Martin knew just when she was needed.

Joan was dreaming that she was at the local hospital. Joan recalled the dream, "I came to a patient's room. Inside the room, I saw my grandmother lying in the hospital bed, and my mother (Mama Martin) was sitting in a chair by the bed. My mother leaned forward and gave me a very stern and disapproving look, the kind of look your mother gives you when you are doing something she does not want you to do. As I was about to step over the threshold and into the room, my mother put her hand on the door and closed the door in my face."

Joan continued with her account, "I turned around and started back up the hall. I looked behind me; it was very dark. I was aware of people moving around in the dark, even though I could not see them. Closer to me, I could see people, but they looked like shadows. I looked ahead toward a light. There was an elevator in the distance, and I moved toward the lighted elevator. As I stepped into the elevator, I woke from sleep. I soon realized that I was having an acute acid reflux attack. It had already progressed to the point where I was choking and struggling to breathe. If I had not dreamed about my mother closing the door, I might have died in my sleep. It felt as though she came to me in the dream and saved my life."

It should be noted that Joan also suffers from (COPD) chronic obstructive pulmonary disease, so breathing is already difficult for her. Had Joan already stopped breathing? Had she already begun to step into the spirit world? Was Mama Martin's stern look a way of telling Joan that she should not be there? Who were the other people in the dream? What was the significance of the lighted elevator? Was it the famous light that many describe in near death experiences? Many questions remain. One thing, however, is certain; a mother's love never dies.

CHAPTER 3

One More Day

Family ties are strong. Losing a loved relative is one of the most difficult events to experience. It is even more difficult to endure when it is a grandparent, mother, father, or sibling. Although most people's religious convictions assure them that they will, one day, be reunited, the immediate sense of loss is still profound. Often, the deceased loved one will return in spirit and give signs to the bereaved family members letting them know they that they are okay and not that far away. In rare instances, those, who are about to transition, are given more time to say their final earthy goodbyes. Such was the case in this remarkable story.

June 23, 1994 is a date that forever changed the life of a young man named Mike. Mike's father, Jim, had been diagnosed with terminal cancer and was receiving hospice care at the family home. On that particular day, hospice workers informed Mike and his mother, Marylyn, that they felt that Jim would pass during the night. He remained in a coma, and his temperature had reached 107 degrees. The hospice staff offered to stay the night, but Marylyn told them to go ahead and leave. She would call them if she needed them. That night, Marylyn stayed up with Jim, waiting on the inevitable. Around 3 a.m., Jim took his last breath and peacefully died. Marylyn stayed with Jim's body and grieved for approximately thirty minutes. She decided to wake Mike and let him know that his father had died. Before she could leave the room, Jim suddenly sat up in bed and asked Marylyn, "Where are you going? I need to talk to you." Needless to say, she was startled; Jim had been in a coma for several days. Before that, he had been so weak that he could not feed himself. Marylyn walked over and sat next to Jim. He said he had begged "them" to let him come back so he could tell his family that he was okay and not to worry about him. He then began to relay messages from passed loved ones.

The first message was from Jim's first wife who had passed away in 1963 from cancer. She was Japanese. Marylyn observed Jim talking to his first wife in Japanese, as if she was there with them. He then would translate the message from his first wife to Marylyn. Jim's first wife thanked Marylyn for taking care of Jim on this side. She then told her that she would take care of him on the other side. Jim told Marylyn that, while he was on the other side, he had talked with relatives and some of his friends who had served with him in Vietnam. He said that the other side was very beautiful; he felt no pain there. Their conversation continued until 7AM when Marylyn insisted that she was going to wake Mike. Surprisingly, Jim asked her to wait until he freshened up. He got up out of bed, on his own, and walked to the bathroom. He showered with no help from Marylyn, who was in shock by what she was witnessing. When Jim said he was ready, Marylyn went to wake Mike. She told him that his father wished to speak to him. Mike was also in shock. He fully expected that his mother was waking him to tell him of his father's passing. Mike walked to the hospice bed, only to find it empty. He then proceeded to his dad's bedroom where he found Jim awake and aware. They spent the next half hour talking. Mike told his Dad "you've had it rough battling cancer for the last 10 years." Jim's response was not what Mike expected to hear. Jim said "I haven't had it rough; Jesus had it rough." Mike was in utter disbelief as he had never heard his dad mention Jesus unless he was cussing. Jim apologized to his son for being so hard on him while he was growing up. Mike told him that it had helped him in his own military career. Jim continued to apologize about other things that he felt he had done wrong in life such as never letting Mike use his tools or showing him how to fix things.

Finally, Jim felt he had said everything he needed to say. He told his family that he needed to go back. Not knowing how that was supposed to work, Marylyn suggested that Jim simply go back to sleep. Mike and Marilyn left Jim and went out into the living room where they talked about what had happened. Around 11 a.m., they heard Jim yell out, "Hello, Hello." They went to check on him. Jim looked very surprised to see them and asked them what they were doing there. He asked them why those on the other side had not come back for him, but they did not have an answer. Marylyn jokingly stated that maybe "they" gave Jim a free pass for the day. "Well I am hungry." Jim blurted out to his surprised family. Jim had been on a liquid diet for almost a month before he fell into a coma. Mike asked him if he wanted a smoothie, some soup, or a milkshake. Jim declined and told them that he wanted a "real meal." He then instructed Mike to get his wallet, go to the store, and buy him something that he would appreciate for dinner. Mike happily obliged. He hastily made his way to the grocery store where he picked out some fresh crawfish, red potatoes, corn on the cob and beer. Mike even picked up a movie just in case his father wanted to watch a movie after they ate.

When Mike arrived home, he found Jim fully dressed and walking around the house. He was even prepping the kitchen to help Mike and Marylyn cook dinner. The family enjoyed a delicious dinner together and then watched the movie that Mike had selected. After the movie, Jim wanted to go back to his bed. Marylyn and Mike stayed with him in the bedroom looking through family photo albums and watching family videos. They talked and shared stories until midnight. By that time, Jim was exhausted and ready to go back to sleep. Marylyn asked him if he wanted to go back to the hospice bed, but he wanted to stay in his own bed. He told them he was going to be fine, and he loved them. In the early hours, Jim once again lapsed into a coma.

The next morning, when the hospice staff arrived, they were upset to find that Jim was out of the hospice bed. When Marylyn and Mike tried to explain what had happened the previous day, the story sounded so incredible that no one believed them. They had no idea how Jim got to his own bed but lectured Mike and his mother about how wrong it was to move him. The hospice staff got a wheel chair and moved Jim back to the hospice bed. At 3 p.m. on June 23, 1994, a day after his birthday, Jim passed away for the second time. Prior to his passing, Jim had told his family that he would try to give them signs from the other side. It seemed that the signs began immediately. As the workers were removing Jim's body, Marylyn and Mike both noticed a beautiful double rainbow in the sky above their house.

On the day of his funeral, Mike offered to make a nice dinner for his mom. The family had a jukebox in their house, and Mike asked if she wanted to listen to the jukebox or watch the news during dinner. Marylyn chose the news. Mike made dinner and brought a plate to his mom in the living room. As Mike was preparing his plate, he heard the sound of the jukebox selecting a record, followed by loud music. Marylyn called out to him and asked why he was playing the jukebox. Mike told his mother that he thought she had turned on the jukebox; she replied that she had not. Somehow, the jukebox had mysteriously started playing by itself. When Mike went to turn the jukebox off, he reached down to hit the off button and was shocked to see that the power cord to the jukebox was lying on the floor. Out of the 100 records in the jukebox, the song that began playing was, "If Tomorrow Never Comes" by Garth Brooks. Mike looked at his Mom and showed her the unplugged cord. He asked her if she thought this was a sign from Dad. As he spoke, the lights on the jukebox dimmed, the record slowed down, and everything stopped.

The afterlife signs from Jim continued. For five consecutive days after Jim passed, a cardinal would arrive at exactly the hour of Jim's death. It would go directly to the window near his hospital bed and peck on the window. On the fifth day, Mike asked his mother if she realized the significance of this occurrence. The cardinal was Jim's favorite bird, and it made its appearance each day at the time of Jim's death. After this recognition, the bird never appeared again.

During the Christmas holiday, Jim once again made his presence known. Mike was Christmas shopping; he bought a large 3 foot tall angel sculpture for Marylyn. As he was loading it into the car, he smelled a very strong odor of cigar smoke. His first thought was that someone was smoking near him. He turned around and saw no one in the parking lot around him. He then heard his Dad's voice in his head. "Hey Mike, you need to go to the

Tokyo market." Mike thought this was just his imagination. He got into his car, and the cigar odor was still prevalent. The aroma reminded Mike of the cigars his dad had smoked during the last years of his life. Mike got goose bumps. Was Jim trying to communicate? Mike certainly felt that he was, so he listened for more messages.

The messages continued with Jim repeating that Mike needed to go to the Tokyo market. At this point, Mike finally answered back and informed Jim that he would go some other time as the market was on the other side of town. He then heard Jim's voice telling him that he had to go there now; he could not wait. As Mike drove to the market, the cigar smell dissipated. When he arrived at the store, the aroma returned. As he proceeded through the door, he again heard the voice of his father. Jim gave him explicit instructions and directed him to an exact location in the store. It was here that he found smoked cuttlefish, one of Jim's favorites. Jim had been waiting years for the store to get the smoked cuttlefish from Japan. Mike gathered all the cuttlefish and proceeded to the register only to be told he could not buy all of it; the market had a loyal customer who had been waiting a long time for them to get this delicacy. The customer's information had been lost, so the store hoped he would come in during the holidays. Mike asked the cashier if she could describe the man who had been waiting for the food. She described Jim. Mike opened his wallet, pulled out a photo of Jim, and showed it to her. Mike asked "Is this the guy?" She replied "Yes, that's him." He then explained to her that his Dad had died in June. The cashier was sorry to hear of Jim's passing and agreed to let Mike buy all the smoked cuttlefish. Mike was pleased. He too loved to eat smoked cuttlefish. As Mike was walking out the door, he once again heard Jim's voice, "Merry Christmas to you and your Mom."

CHAPTER 4

The New Child

Little did he know, as he sat down for lunch, that his life was about to be changed forever. Joe was an innocent five-year old child, when the hands of fate grabbed him and set him on a different journey. It was lunch time; Joe was sitting on a high metal stool eating lunch and drinking a glass of Kool-Aid. During lunch, his grandfather made an unexpected visit. Filled with excitement, Joe rushed to get off the stool to greet his grandfather. In the process, he fell. His glass shattered, and his hand landed on the glass shard nearly severing his left thumb. Blood gushed everywhere. His mother attempted to stop the bleeding but was unsuccessful. Joe was rushed to the hospital. According to Joe's mother, there happened to be a German doctor who was visiting the hospital on that particular day. The German doctor made the comment that he thought he could reattach the thumb and save the young boy. Joe's mother could barely understand the foreign doctor but was desperate for help and agreed.

Joe was rushed into surgery. During the surgery, Joe left his body. "I felt weightless," Joe recalled. "I floated up to a corner of the operating room. I looked down, and I could see the doctors and the nurses working on me." He did not understand what was happening. He was looking at himself which confused him, but he felt no fear. Joe continued to describe his experience, "It was the most serene experience that I've ever had. I've never felt anything near that again." He remarked further, "It's nothing to be afraid of. Everything is going to be fine." Joe has no memory of seeing a tunnel of light as is often described by those who've had an NDE. Instead, what he saw was similar to the picture on an old tube television set, where the light would slowly fade to a little point then blink out. Joe was resuscitated but fell into a coma after the surgery. Years later, his mother told him that the nurses checked on him regularly during those early hours; they did not think he was going to survive due to extreme blood loss.

While comatose, Joe had vivid memories of being somewhere other than his hospital bed. He remembered being in a large building reminiscent of 1930's architecture. He recalled the experience, "I don't know where the light came from, but there was a really bright, white light everywhere. There was a lady who was dressed like a nurse in a white dress complete with the old style nurse's hat. Every day she would come for me, and we would walk around the building. I was allowed to look out the windows, but I was never allowed to go outside." Joe said that every time he looked out the window, it was overcast outside, like a rainy spring day. Other than the gloomy weather, everything else looked nice; it looked like a park. He also saw other people there. They were walking down these small paths. These people looked normal and were dressed in attire that fit present day fashion.

Joe continued, "The lady was always telling me things, but I can only re-member the last thing she told me. During my last walk with her she said, 'It's not for you. It's time to go back.' I always knew that there were other people in the building with me because I could hear other voices. I never saw them, but I knew they were there. The nurse was the only one I actually ever saw other than the ones outside the window." Joe feels that the building he was in was a sort of stopping place for souls before cross-ing over. He feels that the ones he saw outside in the park like setting had already crossed over. That is why he was not allowed to go outside. As the nurse had told him, "It's not for you." It was not Joe's time to die. He was a young boy with a lot of living yet to do.

Soon after, Joe regained consciousness and made a full recovery. He was given exercises to regain the strength in his injured hand. He was instructed to do these exercises with both hands which made him ambidextrous. It was during this time, that weird stuff started happening. Joe recalled the first strange event, "I was sitting on the porch one day, and I decided to draw my dad's car. I had an old tablet and a pencil. They had me writing and drawing a lot, anything to exercise the hand. My Dad had an old 1949 Plymouth, and that's what I drew. There was no doubt about it. I drew a 49 Plymouth. I had no idea that I could do that and neither did anybody else!" Joe was only five years old at the time. Before Joe started school at age six, he was already reading, writing, and doing advanced drawing. When he did start school, Joe was well advanced over the other children his age.

By the time Joe entered third grade, his teacher suggested that he leave public school and enroll in a school for gifted children. His family lived in the Nashville, Tennessee area, and at the time, the only school in the city for gifted children was a Catholic school. Joe's parents were not Catholic and did not want to send him to a Catholic school, so he remained in the public school system. As he aged, his interest expanded into subjects that were of little interest to children his age. He felt isolated and alone. Joe spent many hours reading in the back corners of the local library; he was a self-described, "nerd." Joe was especially advanced in science and electronics. He would learn, not only, to program computers but to build them as well. He was, and remains to this day, fascinated by aerospace, science, and astronomy.

Although he does not remember that much about his personality prior to the accident, Joe believes that his NDE changed him. He came back with new abilities in art, music and even psychic gifts. Somehow, his IQ increased or was enhanced by his experience. These changes were profound. His entire demeanor and personality changed too, which was very noticeable to both friends and family. "My Mom and other people told me that there was a personality change when I came back. She said it was like one person went into the hospital, but somebody different came back."

Another odd occurrence happened recently when Joe went to an event to see a medium. The event was held at a local theater and was well attended. During the course of the audience reading, Joe was singled out which took him by surprise. The medium said that Joe's mother was speaking to her.

She began to tell Joe many thing that she had no way of knowing. She told Joe that his mother had always been concerned about him because she knew that he was different. She, however, did not know what to do about it other than to keep Joe safe and out of trouble. She also knew that Joe had experienced a lot of anguish because he was not like the other kids. The medium then told Joe that "he wasn't always like this; something had made him this way." She also attributed his change to his NDE; she felt that Joe had psychic abilities like hers but had not yet learned how to use them.

At first, Joe was surprised to hear what the medium told him about his own psychic abilities. After the event, he started thinking about what she had told him. It was then that he remembered some unusual incidents relating to her message. Joe recalled one such incident, "I was going to Business College at night and working at an auto parts warehouse during the day. Sometime around lunch one day, I climbed up a ladder to put some stock on a shelf. As I was climbing down the ladder, I got so dizzy. It was like I was spinning around. I thought I was going to fall off the ladder. I made it to the bottom of the ladder and immediately sat down. I felt a strong jolt, like an electric shock go through me. Then a strong sense of awareness came over me. I knew something bad had happened, and I knew it involved my grandfather." Joe continued, "About five minutes after that, I got paged to the front of the warehouse. My Mom had called; she wanted me to come pick her up and take her to the hospital. She said that my grandfather had had an accident. My grandfather, who worked in construction, was on the roof of a two story house and had fallen. He had busted up one of his legs, and they were rushing him to the hospital. I asked when it happened, and she told me that it couldn't have been more than five or ten minutes ago. I then realized that was when I had the dizzy spell and the sensation of falling. Maybe the jolt, I felt, was when he hit the ground."

Another strange thing that Joe has experienced since his NDE is precognitive dreaming. These dreams are easily distinguished from other dreams. Joe will wake up sweating and be very tired. They are vivid with great detail. "I will be someplace that I don't know" Joe explained. "I will walk through the building, but no one can see me. I know where everything is located in the building. I know who everyone is. Then weeks or even months later, I will go somewhere that I've never been. When I arrive, I instantly recognize the place from my dream. I will know where all the rooms are and already know some of the peoples' names who work there." Joe said that he also had these kinds of dreams as a child. "It would freak my Mom out. We moved a lot, so I had to change schools every couple of years. There were times, when we went to register, I would tell my Mom, 'I know this place. We need to go in here, go to the right, and go down two doors; there's a guy in there to help us.' If I already knew the names of those we needed to see, it would freak her out even more. Occasionally, that happened."

Because of his near death experience and all the high strangeness that has surrounded him throughout his life, Joe sought answers. That quest led him to a keen interest in the paranormal. "I thought it was fascinating." Joe said. "I read everything I could on the subject. I talked to everyone I could to learn more. "Somebody once made the comment to me that I didn't have any sense. What most people were running from, I was running towards. I had to know the answers. Even now, I still need answers." Joe continued, "It always seemed to me that there was just one key piece of information missing. If I could ever find it, it would put all this stuff in perspective. It's like the unified field theory; there's always that one key that is just within reach. If you can ever find it, you have all the answers." In retrospect, Joe now thinks that we are not meant to know all the answers while in this plane of existence. They will be revealed when we transition to the other side. "It's kind of like quantum mechanics. It's all probability," Joe said. "Everything exists in the same space and time simultaneously. It's just that somehow we select and manifest the reality around us. If someone actually knew how that worked, they could probably reshape everything."

Joe's connection with the spirit world did not subside once he returned. Since then, he has seen spirits of humans and animals. This occurs through his peripheral vision. When he turns to look at them directly, they disappear. Often, he will hear them speaking to him. In the past, he would tell others about it only to be told that he was crazy; now he does not speak about it. This spirit communication does not bother him. It has been ongoing his entire life, and he considers it normal regardless of others' opinions. Joe is also an empath. He strongly feels the energy and emotions of other people. Sometimes, this ability results in panic attacks or severe anxiety when he is around large groups of people because he becomes inundated with so many emotions at once. Undoubtedly, these things are what the medium meant when she told Joe that he too was like her.

As one might expect, Joe's NDE changed his view of death. He has used his experience and perception of what happens when we die to help others. Joe said, "I've talked to people about that a lot; because over the course of the last ten years, my wife and I have lost all of our parents, grandparents, a ton of friends and other family members. I've talked to other people in hospice. They all are afraid of death. I tell them that there is nothing to be afraid of. The only thing you need to be concerned about is the method in which you die. The experience itself is a beautiful thing. I've never felt anything so peaceful. I'm not afraid of death, and I tell people that they shouldn't be afraid of it either. It's only a transition."

CHAPTER 5

Death in the Desert

1993 is a year that Hector will never forget; it was almost the last year of his life. Hector was in the military and was stationed in Fort Louis, Washington. In the spring of 1993, he was sent to the desert near Bartow, California to be part of a training exercise. To get to the remote desert, the soldiers traveled by train. This train, however, was no ordinary transport train. There was no seating. It was more like a livestock train; the men were forced to stand for the trip. As the trip progressed, Hector noticed that smoke was entering the railway car through a hole near him. After a few minutes of inhaling this smoke, Hector began to feel sick.

Hector recalled, "It was about 5 A.M. when we arrived at the desert training facility. By this time, I had a huge headache. I had been standing near the hole and inhaling the fumes the entire trip. We hadn't slept the whole night. We finally got the green light to take a rest, so I lay down in desert. I had never been to the desert before and did not realize how quickly it heats up once the sun comes up." Hector continued, "When I woke up, I was very hot, and I had the worst migraine of my life. I was seeing flashes of light and was very nauseated. I asked one of my friends to take me to the medical treatment facility that they were setting up in the desert. I couldn't see well enough to walk there by myself, so he guided me by the hand and led me there. When I got there, they asked what was going on with me. I told them about my headache. 'Are you nauseated?' They asked. I told them that I was. They then gave me an injection of Compazine. I didn't know it at the time, but I was allergic to it."

Hector had a severe reaction to the Compazine. He went into cardiac arrest right after the injection. The attending doctor and nurses administered CPR. It worked, and his heart began beating again. When he regained consciousness, he asked the doctor what had happened; he was told that he had gone into cardiac arrest. As Hector was being transferred to the main base hospital, the doctor instructed the ambulance attendants to give Hector more Compazine so that he would not vomit in the ambulance. He was given another injection of Compazine, which, once again, caused him to go into cardiac arrest. "This time I found myself floating above everybody," Hector said. "I was above my own body and higher than everyone else. There were a lot of people working on me. I could see the names on the uniforms of all the different people working on me. I could hear everything they were saying. I could see everything in great detail. I looked at my body; I could see that I was completely unconscious and not breathing. I saw them rush to get a crash cart to shock my heart."

Hector described how he felt, "At that moment, I felt completely at peace and happy. I was feeling love like I had never experienced before or since. I looked at my body, and I told myself 'We are always wondering when and where we are going to die. You died here in the desert, and you died from a heart attack.' I was fine with that. Then I looked to my left, and I saw this shiny light. It wasn't a tunnel, but it felt like I was already in a tunnel looking at a light." He continued, "I felt like I wanted to go to that light. It was like the light was pulling me, but it was a subtle pull that I could control. I knew if I let myself, I would go towards that light. I was having trouble resisting it; I wanted to let myself go. It was at that moment that I remembered that I was married and had just had my first daughter. I knew that I couldn't go and leave them alone to struggle by themselves. I looked down at my body again. They were giving me the electrical shocks, and I wasn't responding. I told myself, 'you are dying because you aren't breathing.' 'Why don't you breathe?' Then the feeling of wanting to go to the light grew even stronger. The closer I moved towards the light, the more I wanted to go into the light. I was torn between my desire to go to the light or stay in my earthly body. It was a very strange experience. I could see my lifeless body below me, and I could see myself as a spirit. I was dressed the same way in both realities. It was like I was a hologram of myself; I was, somewhat, translucent but also, somewhat, solid. Finally, I told myself to breathe. Instantly, I found myself inside my physical body, and I was breathing. They then loaded me into the ambulance and gave me another shot of Compazine, and I went into cardiac arrest for the third time."

The doctors and nurses did not realize that Compazine was causing Hector to go into cardiac arrest. They had administered several drugs and failed to recognize which drug was causing the cardiac arrest. The EMTs quickly used the paddles on Hector and brought him back once again. Hector was admitted to the hospital and kept overnight for observation. The next day, he was released. He returned to duty, even though he was having difficulty breathing and still not feeling well. Hector was given medication to help his breathing. Although not easy, he remained at the desert training facility for the next 30 days.

Hector was a religious man before his NDE. His experience with the after-life changed both his perception of life and his religious beliefs. He said, "I am very skeptical by nature. I have a scientific mind. I have to see and touch something; things have to be proven. After my NDE, I started digging into my experience to try and understand what had happened to me. I started reading about near death experiences and how they happen. Science says that an NDE happens because of a lack of oxygen to the brain. I understand what they are saying. Yes, some people might conduct experiments that can induce a near death experience or something close to it and derive that theory. However, that's not what happened to me. I believe that my consciousness was, somehow, out of my body. It had a form; it even had clothing. I had my eyes closed, and, yet, I could see everything."

Hector continued with how his NDE had affected him. "It did not make me religious. It made me think that what religion teaches, about life after death, is not quite right. I didn't believe in the literal concept of Heaven or Hell. To me, the light that I saw and felt was not like going to Heaven. It was more like becoming part of the universe. I felt like I was going to be pure energy. I was going to be part of a major amount of energy or the universe. That feeling, of being a part of pure energy, liberated me from any physical pain. I felt like I was going to dissolve in it and no longer be a part of the consciousness I was on earth. It was an excellent feeling. I have no words to properly describe how good it felt. The closer I got to the light, the better it felt. I felt no fear or pain. I felt only deep love and deep happiness like I had never experienced before and haven't experienced since. Had it not been for my strong sense of duty to my family, I would have gladly gone into the light."

Hector did not feel like his NDE was a religious experience; it was not about going to heaven or hell. It was more of a metaphysical experience and not like how he had been taught by his Christian upbringing. Since his brush with the other side, Hector no longer fears death. He elaborated, "Since then, I have completely lost a fear of death. When I was in the military, I was sent to Iraq for a year. I knew I was going to go and do what I had to do. If something happened and I was killed, then I was okay with it. I knew that there was no pain in dying." Another change that came over Hector, after his death in the desert, was his desire to be a better person. "I began to try to live my life the best that I could. Up to that point, I was just living. I started to organize my life. I did what I needed to do so that when I do die again, I won't have to come back. My life has changed in many ways. I have realized that there is no perfection, but I have tried the best I could to fulfill my purpose and duty. Part of my purpose was preparing my family to carry on in my absence. If I die again, they will be fine without me, and I will not have that strong sense of duty to come back like the last time. I do not want to have any remorse in that state of being."

The lessons of his near death experience helped Hector cope when he was dealt one of life's cruelest blows; he lost his youngest daughter in a car crash when she was only 18. He related that tragic day, "The day my daughter died was a Friday. I have PTSD from the war, and, almost every night, I have nightmares. That night, however, with all the craziness and all the shock, I fell asleep. I wasn't having any dreams. Then, my daughter came to me. It was like she was in a kind of fog. I heard her giggling. She said, 'Hey Daddy, remember the conversations we had before, and you said that we probably didn't go anywhere when we die? Well, we do go to a place, and I'm doing fine. You will be fine too, when your time comes.' She was very happy. I didn't feel that that was a dream. Somehow, she got the chance to let me know that she was okay. She knew that I needed to hear that from her; it gave me peace. I still have pain that she is gone, but I know that she is doing fine wherever she is. I know that she is happy."

Obviously, Hector's view and perspective of the death process are different than most people. We can, however, learn from him and others, who have crossed over and returned. He offers an important piece of advice, "Before you die, you need to live your life the best that you can. Do the things you want and need to do, so that you feel accomplished. You need to be at peace, when your time comes. Death is the best feeling that you can ever experience. If you die and you stay in that state forever, it's wonderful." He concludes, "Imagine being everywhere, seeing everything, and experiencing everything all at the same time in total peace and happiness; this is what awaits us on the other side."

Chapter 6

My Baby, My Life

Manuela was only seventeen when she got married. To her surprise, she soon found out she was pregnant. Although very young, she was determined to keep the child and be the best mother possible. Unfortunately, something went wrong with her pregnancy, and Manuela experienced an ectopic pregnancy. Ectopic pregnancy occurs when the embryo implants somewhere other than the uterus. It is a serious condition and requires emergency treatment due to the possibility of fallopian tube rupture and severe bleeding. Manuela was rushed to the hospital and placed in intensive care. After examining her, Manuela's doctor informed her of the seriousness of her condition. She was told that the baby could not be saved.

By this time, some of her family members had arrived at the hospital to be with her. Not fully understanding the severity of her condition and wanting to be with her family, she asked to be removed from intensive care and taken to a regular room. Her request was denied. While visiting with one of her relatives, Manuela found herself becoming weaker and weaker. Her pain was so severe that she began going in and out of consciousness. "I remember that my cousin told me afterwards that everybody in the hospital was shocked because I was crying and shouting out, 'Don't do me harm. Don't do me harm.' Even today I still wonder why I was shouting like that. Why was I so afraid?"

"I wanted to be a Mommy so badly," Manuela explained. "After the horrendous experience of my first pregnancy, my doctor told me, 'You cannot try again. It is a miracle that you are alive. If you try again, this time you will die.' I didn't care. I wanted a baby more than anything. After that warning from her doctor, Manuela had a vivid dream. In this dream she was in a hospital. Everything was white. She saw a man who looked like he had nylons pulled over his head, as if he was a bank robber. The man yelled out, 'I will kill you all.' Before the dream ended, Manuela saw one last image. "I saw a white pigeon in my dream," Manuela said. "It gave me hope. It gave me courage to try again, so I did."

Unfortunately, this time was no different than Manuela's first pregnancy. Her doctor had been right, and she found herself back in the hospital. She was in severe pain, as she was being rushed through the hallways of the hospital. Manuela described what happened, "I remember passing by room after room. I could see my brothers beside me. I could see how panicked they were. Then someone injected me with a very big needle; I blacked out. The next thing I remember was being in a room; I had left my body. My mother was in front of me; the doctor was a few steps away, and he was writing my death certificate. My mother asked him to give me something to bring me back, which he did. However, I was still out of my body. I saw him ask a nurse if she would donate blood to me. She told him that she was menstruating and felt it was too dangerous for her to do so. The doctor told her, 'yes, it can be a bit dangerous, but you will not die from it. If she doesn't get blood, this young girl will die.' The nurse then agreed to give me blood. It saved my life."

The doctor then called for an ambulance to transport Manuela to a larger hospital where she could receive more extensive treatment. Manuela was still out of her body. She recalled what happened next, "I was in the ambulance; it was red. All the doors were shut. On the way to the hospital, the ambulance was involved in an accident. The EMTs got out. I was still out of my body, so I followed them. A young man was involved in the accident. They told him that they could not help him because they had a 17 year old girl who they were trying to save. The last thing I consciously remember was waking up in the hospital and seeing a nurse. I asked her if she was real. I didn't know if I was waking up on the other side or if I was seeing her because of the anesthesia. She looked at me with an angry look on her face, and then I blacked out once again."

Manuela explained how she felt while out of her body. "I did not feel any pain. All the extreme pain that I had was gone." She said, "I felt like I was everywhere, all at the same time. I have never forgotten that incredible feeling; I know I never will." Manuela already was a believer in life after death, at the time of her experience. As a child, she spent a large amount of time with her grandmother who instilled those beliefs in her. Manuela's NDE merely confirmed and validated those beliefs. She cannot say with certainty where we go when we die; since she did not fully cross over. She is, however, certain that our soul leaves our physical body, at the time of death. She knows we continue on.

Like so many others who have shared their near death experience, Manuela returned with psychic gifts. Because of where she was born, she has never felt comfortable using these gifts. Manuela explained, "I am highly empathic and feel energy from both people and places. I can feel people and their energy or their vibration, so to speak. If I feel negativity or low vibration from a person, I will avoid them. On the other hand, if I feel good energy, I know that I will be okay around them. It seems that people are attracted to me in such a way that even complete strangers approach me. For instance, if I am taking a walk and see people who aren't happy, they will start talking to me. They will unload all of their misery and suffering of their life onto me. I listen and try to tell them that it will get better, but, afterwards, I am the one who is drained from absorbing all of their negative energy."

Manuela's brief foray to the other side also caused her to gain a keen interest in the paranormal. She studied all that she could on the many facets of the subject. Her interest in the paranormal was such that, at one time, she wanted to become a parapsychologist. It was very difficult for her to find books on the subject where she lived because the libraries did not carry these books. Still, she has persevered. She has found many answers and connected with others, who have come back from death with similar accounts. To this day, she still has frequent psychic and paranormal experiences. She lives without fear of them, and she lives without fear of death.

She has learned to appreciate life. She knows that she has been given a second chance. You see, Manuela's interpretation of the dove that appeared in her dream was correct. She trusted the message so much that she was willing to risk her health to become pregnant. The risk was worth it for Manuela. She was able to give birth to a healthy baby boy. She is now both a mother and a grandmother.

CHAPTER 7

Unrestful Souls

It is said that love of money is the root of evil. While that is a subjective idea, we do often see examples of it. Sometimes, the love of money causes people to do heinous things. That appears to have happened in a small town in eastern Kentucky. Residents believe that homes, in a particular neighborhood, were built on the grounds of a former cemetery. Using burial ground for new housing development, in and of itself, is not uncommon. Developers are given permission to relocate the graves from their current location. Most of the time, this is done in a professional and respectful manner. There have been times, however, when greed and profit have taken precedent. In an effort to cut costs and increase profit, a company might, simply, move the headstones and build over the top of the still occupied graves. This not only happens with regular cemeteries but with ancient Native American burial grounds as well. Although it has never been proven, it appears that this is what happened in this sad case, creating unrest among the dead buried there.

Maria is a seasoned paranormal investigator. She is not the kind you see on "reality ghost shows." Rather, she is pragmatic and level-headed, a consummate professional who takes her work seriously. Maria is a member of a small paranormal team. When the team heard about a reported haunting in the aforementioned neighborhood, they went to investigate. They were anxious to find the cause of the unusual paranormal activity at the house, which had been so severe that the owner had moved. The team had the proper equipment, and they had years of experience in the field. If the reported haunting was genuine, they would find and document it.

Maria's team learned as much as they could about the house before the investigation. The owner had seen the house for sale and wanted to buy it for him and his wife. The couple spent a few days mulling over their decision. During this time, the man's wife discovered that a family member had previously owned the house. They decided to buy it. Not long after they moved in, however, things got ominous. They felt continuous negativity in the house and began to fight constantly. The man fell into a deep depression and started to exhibit aggressive behavior. This eventually took a toll on the marriage, and his wife left him. After she left, the man got a dog. While away from home, the man kept the dog in the large basement. When he would return home, he would let the dog out of the basement. The poor animal was always terrified. After only three days together, the man let the dog out of the basement and took him outside for a walk. The dog was so upset that he ran directly into traffic and was killed instantly. To this day, claw marks remain on that basement door.

Maria recalled more of the owner's tragic story, "Whatever was in that house constantly tormented him. He would go to bed at night, and this thing would wake him by tapping above his head. It would quit when he would wake up. When he would go back to sleep, it would do it again. He never got any sleep. His anger got so bad that he punched holes in the bathroom wall." Maria continued, "It got so bad that he attempted suicide. He even tried to kill whatever it was that was incessantly haunting him. There were bullet holes in the floor, where he tried to shoot it. It was driving him mad. He eventually ended up in the hospital and never returned to live in the house."

When the team arrived, they were shocked as they entered the house. "When we walked in, we saw that somebody had nailed crosses all over the house," Maria explained. The team continued on about their business and set up their gear for the investigation. It did not take long before strange things started happening. Maria recalled one of the first incidents, "Whatever was in that house would control the thermostat on the air conditioning unit. It was a digital thermostat. I know that those things can be set to come on at certain times and go up or down, but this was different. It happened repeatedly. We would be in a room doing an EVP (electronic voice phenomena) session, and, all of a sudden, we would realize that it was getting very hot in the house. The thermostat had been set at 73 degrees. When we went to check it, the temperature setting had been moved to 85 degrees. We examined the thermostat and discovered that it was not set on a timer. The temperature setting had to have been moved deliberately by something. Later that evening, we went down to the basement. We turned off the air conditioning unit so that our digital recorders would not pick up the sound of air moving through the duct work. While we were down there, the air conditioner suddenly came back on. No one on my team turned it on. No one was even upstairs at the time."

The paranormal activity continued throughout the night. The team's cameras repeatedly malfunctioned for no apparent reason. They did manage to record several EVPs at the house as well as numerous readings on their K2 meters, which measure and detect electromagnetic frequencies. It is believed that the energy of a ghost can be detected with these kinds of EMF meters. Maria had an unusual incident while using her K2 meter that night. "I was walking through the house with a K2 meter. Every time I would turn around to back track, the lights on my K2 would go crazy. It was like someone was following me." Another team member was using a thermal camera, which measures and photographs heat signatures. On it, she captured an image of a humanoid figure that appeared to be wearing a Native American head dress. It definitely seemed as though the house was occupied by several ghosts, for the paranormal team members heard multiple disembodied voices throughout the night. They also witnessed shadow figures moving about the house.

At about 2 A.M, Maria felt herself becoming extremely tired. She decided to lie down in the bedroom the owner had used, as the bed was still there. As she began to doze off, she heard a tapping sound coming from above her head. When she opened her eyes, the tapping would stop. As soon as she would close her eyes and almost fall asleep, the tapping sound would start again. She got up to investigate the sound. The room, directly above her, was carpeted, so no one could be tapping on the floor. Besides, there was no one in that room. She went back to bed and tried to relax. Then, out of nowhere, a little girl appeared. Maria recalled the incident, "a little girl wearing a night gown came into my room. She walked right past me and went into the bathroom. She had on a long sleeve night gown with pin stripes and flowers on it. She had shoulder length blond hair and looked to be about 9 to 12 years old. She seemed completely unaware of me. I was very tired and, at first, didn't realize what I had seen because she looked so real. I actually waited for a few minutes, expecting her to come out of the bathroom. Then, as I gathered my thoughts, I realized that the light had not been turned on. I immediately got up to tell my team what had happened. We all wondered if the owner had also seen the ghost of the young girl. Maybe, that was what finally sent him over the edge."

It was not just the house that was affected by something negative dwelling within its walls. It appeared that other residences and even a business in the area were as well. "There was a convenience store three houses down; they had shootings and fights at that store all the time." Maria further described the area, "There was a cemetery within walking distance of the house we investigated. The lady, who lived in the house next door, kept her lights on all night long, every night. The people, who lived in the house behind this one, had paranormal activity in the front part of their house but not in the bedrooms or back part of the house." Maria's team and other paranormal investigators believed that, at least, part of the neighborhood was built over the tops of graves. The headstones were moved, but the bodies remained. It was also suspected that some of the land was sacred Native American burial ground. Because of this, the souls buried there cannot rest. As a result, they continue to haunt unsuspecting intruders and scare them away, so they can, once again, rest in peace.

CHAPTER 8

Echoes of War

The echoes of war ring loud and long. War ravages everything in its path, leaving scars that never heal. Its effects, like tentacles, reach generation after generation. The wounds of war can be so severe that even death cannot mend these broken souls. The United States has fought only one war on its own soil—the Civil War. Although named the Civil War, it proved to be anything but civil. To this day, there are places in the United States where remnants of our great war still linger, places where it is as if time has stood still. These locations are not just the battlefields, where countless brave soldiers fought and died but also the buildings and homes that happened to be in the wrong place at the wrong time and are forever etched into the fabric of time. They are places of great sadness, suffering, and hardship. One such place is Octagon Hall in Franklin, Kentucky.

Octagon Hall, present day.
Photo courtesy of Maria Duff Wilson

This antebellum, eight-sided, three story brick home was built in 1847. The owner, Andrew Jackson Caldwell, resided there with his family. When the Civil War began, Mr. Caldwell fully supported the Confederacy. When the famous "orphan brigade" fled Bowling Green, Kentucky in February of 1862, they marched south, eventually ending up at the Caldwell home. It has been estimated that eight to nine thousand Confederate troops set up camp on the property. It was during this time that the home became a hospital for the troops, and it remained a hospital throughout the war. Not long after the Confederate troops left, five thousand Union troops descended upon the Caldwell residence and forced the Caldwell family to tend to their needs. The Union soldiers were cruel to both the Caldwell family and the slaves; these atrocities were not soon forgotten. After the Union troops left, word circulated that Confederate soldiers were welcome at Octagon Hall. They were assured food, shelter, and medical care. Secret rooms and tunnels were built for the sole purpose of hiding Confederate soldiers, should the Union forces show up looking for them. Over the years, the family experienced its share of personal tragedy. There were deaths in the family, but one of the most tragic was the death of Andrew's 12 year

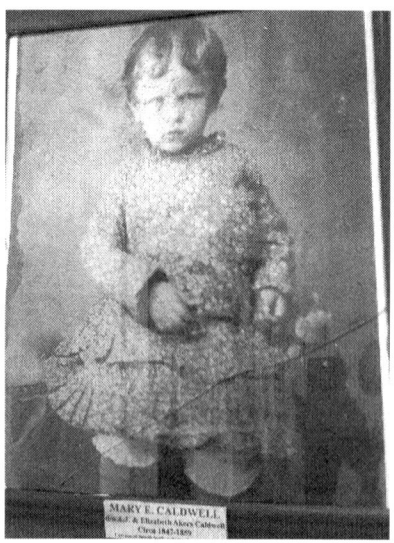

Elizabeth Caldwell
Photo courtesy of Maria Duff Wilson.

old daughter, Mary Elizabeth. There have been conflicting accounts as to what happened to her in that winter kitchen. What is known is that, somehow, her dress caught fire from the fireplace. She suffered extensive injuries, languished for seven days, and finally died from the burns. Whether she accidently fell or was pushed into the fireplace has been a matter of speculation for years.

Over time, Octagon Hall has garnered the reputation of being one of the most haunted locations in the south. Ghostly sightings have included Civil War soldiers, slaves, and Caldwell family members, including Mary Elizabeth. With such a rich and dark history, it is no surprise that the house would be crawling with paranormal activity. Even the octagon shape of the house is considered a conduit for spirit activity in the occult. Octagon Hall has been featured on numerous national television shows. Unlike so many other historic locations, the curator of the Octagon Hall museum, Billy Byrd, does not try to keep the haunting a secret. In fact, it is whole heartedly promoted. Due to its well earned reputation as one of the most haunted homes in the south, many ghost hunting teams have investigated Octagon Hall. Maria's team, discussed in chapter six, is one such group; they act as resident hosts there. In addition to having investigated the house and grounds many times, her team also keeps IR surveillance cameras running 24 hours a day. Over the years, they have caught unexplainable phenomena with their equipment. They also have conducted novice ghost hunts at various times throughout the year. Maria has seen people run out of Octagon Hall during an investigation. Most are so scared that they vow never to return.

Some of these people have experienced a menacing ghost, who has a penchant for attacking men. "I believe it's a man shadow person because I don't think a woman would be that big," Maria said. "Once, while I was guiding a novice ghost hunt, he confronted me. I was standing in what we call the 'sick room,' one of the main rooms used as a hospital room during the war. The 'sick room' is large with two doors. On this particular night, I was standing by one of the doors. A young couple sat directly across from me on one of the beds. We had just started an EVP session, hoping to get some spirit communication. I was standing and looking in the direction of the other door, which was on the other side of the room.

All of a sudden, I saw the head of a shadow person peek around the corner. It moved into the doorway and took up the entire space of the doorway. It wasn't as tall as the top of the door frame, but it was huge!" Maria exclaimed. "It then walked into the room. Since the home is now a museum, there are artifacts, display cases, and antique furniture throughout the house. The shadow man walked right though a bed and stood directly in front of me. It was blacker than black. I could no longer see the young couple, sitting across from me. One of them made the comment, 'I can't see you anymore.' It was right in front of me, and I was looking up at it. I felt, what I can only describe as, an electrical charge over my entire body. My hair stood on end! Thankfully, after facing me for a few seconds, it turned and walked out into the hall. Even though I never felt threatened, I was happy when he left. This ghost, apparently, comes around to see if a visitor is male or female. He's never attacked a female, but a number of men have reported being attacked and chased out of the house. They have reported feeling like they were having a heart attack; they couldn't breathe. They knew they had to get out of that house."

It seems that the ghosts of Octagon Hall never rest. "You can't walk into that place and not have an experience," Maria said. She related an experience that happened during a recent novice ghost hunt. "It was Halloween night of 2017. The event was to begin at 6 PM. By the time I left work and got there, it was almost 6:00. Everyone, attending the ghost hunt, had gathered outside. One of my team members was talking to them and telling them how the hunt would work. The team also offered some ghost hunting tips. As the orientation continued, I made my way into the house and said, 'Hello Caldwell's how are you today?' This was my usual introduction when entering the house. I, then, put my stuff down and started to unpack. Shortly thereafter, the novice ghost hunters began to enter the house. I thought that I should turn on all the lights, so everyone could tour the house first. As I got to the top of the stairs, I immediately noticed the door to Mary Elizabeth's room was closed. This was very odd because that door was never closed. After I finished turning on all the lights, I went back downstairs and told a team member about the door. We had infrared cameras running continuously throughout the house, so we checked the camera that was monitoring that particular room. At 5:45 that evening, the door closed all by itself. This was also about the same time that I drove into the driveway."

The security cameras have picked up numerous unexplainable incidents over the years. Various objects have been caught moving. Recently, an un-explainable light appeared above a candelabra. It looked as though a can-dle was lit, but there were no candles. Maria stated that various incidents have occurred, involving the motion sensors on the museum's display cases. "There have been times that, as soon as we got to the back door and before entering the house, the motion sensors would trigger and come on. The displays are inside a room on the other side of the house. There is no reason for them to come on." Maria continued, "The police have told us that they have been across from the house and have witnessed the motion sensor lights come on in the middle of the night, even though there was clearly no one in the house. These kinds of events have happened so many times that it has become a joke of sorts with the local police. When Billy Byrd, the museum curator, took over Octagon Hall, he had an alarm installed. Three or four times a week, he would get calls from the Sheriff's Department tell-ing him that the alarms were going off. They would meet Billy but would not step one foot into that house, not even when Billy was with them."

The haunting of Octagon Hall has not been restricted to the house. There have been many reports of ghostly activity on the surrounding property, including the barn and the slave cemetery. Maria's husband, Jimmy, has had very strange interactions with a ghost in the slave cemetery. "Every time we have gone to the house, Jimmy has gone out to the slave cemetery and placed a flashlight near one particular grave. Since the slaves only had rocks for headstones, he placed the flashlight on a rock. He then introduced himself and asked, 'would you like some smoking tobacco?' Every time he did this, the flashlight turned on. He then told the ghost to turn off the flashlight, and he would bring him some tobacco. Invariably, the flashlight turned off. He, then, lit a cigarette and set it on the headstone. When Jimmy asked the ghost if he was enjoying it, the flashlight came back on."

There have been other incidents of high strangeness in the slave cemetery. Maria recalled one such incident. On one particular day, she was in the cemetery conducting an EVP session. As she started to leave, she heard a very high pitched tone in her ear. This tone was so loud that it actually hurt her ears, and she remarked out loud about it. Later, when going over the audio from the recorder, she heard her comment about the tone, and, right after that, she caught an EVP of, what sounded like, an old black man. The forlorn voice, from the other side, said, "Help me." Maria believed this voice to be a deceased slave. Perhaps, he is still trapped and still believes he is enslaved.

Another incident of spirit communication also happened in the cemetery. "About three weeks ago, some of my team had taken a group of guests out to the slave cemetery. I had my 'ghost box' turned on. One of the guys, from my team, told me to walk over to Emma's grave. Emma was a slave girl, who died young. I said, 'I don't remember where her grave is.' He told me to walk over towards it, and he would tell me when to stop. I walked towards the grave, and, suddenly, through the ghost box, I heard 'Right here!'"

The ghosts, in the house, appear to like certain people more than others. This is often seen when groups tour the house. "If there is one person in the group that the ghosts don't like, nothing paranormal will happen. When we split them into smaller groups, the person's group, who they don't like, will have nothing happen. The other group will have all kinds of experiences. We really don't know why there are some people that they don't like or seem to want there." Maria related. "The ghosts of Octagon Hall really seem to detest children. Every time a school group comes through the house, something will break. We've had a water line burst, and we've had the breakers blown. It always coincides with children being there."

Maria and her paranormal team have spent countless hours investigating Octagon Hall. Through personal experiences and by using their equipment, they have learned the identities of many of the ghost that still reside there. There is Jerome Clark, whose gun is on display in the museum. Maria said that he was known to dress up like a woman and even had the nickname of "Sue Mundy." He, apparently, does not like to be called by his nickname and gets upset if anyone refers to him by it. Another familiar ghost is a man they call "Eddie." He can be heard dragging his injured leg across the floor. Eddie has communicated with Maria's team through EVP. He told them that he was shot by a Union soldier and came to the house seeking refuge. As Union soldiers approached the house, the Caldwell family hid him in the attic, where he remained for three days. When the Union soldiers finally left, the family rushed to the attic to check on Eddie. He, unfortunately, had succumbed to his injuries. It appears, however, that Eddie may not be aware of his death and is still hiding in the attic, waiting for help.

The ghost of the Caldwells' daughter, Mary Elizabeth, is one of the most active souls that remain on the property. Many people have seen, heard, or felt her gentle presence. Maria, once, felt Mary Elizabeth grab her by the arm, hold her for a short time, and then let go. Balls in Mary Elizabeth's bedroom have been seen rolling on their own. Someone will roll a ball across the floor and ask Mary Elizabeth to roll it back. The ball will then, slowly, roll back to the person from which it came. It seems that the girl, who crossed over at such a young age, still enjoys playing. Billy Byrd saw a full body apparition of a young girl, who he believes was Mary Elizabeth. One afternoon, while in the basement winter kitchen, he saw a girl that looked so real that he thought a tourist had stopped by the house. When he spoke to the little girl, asking if he could help, she turned away from him, encapsulated herself, and disappeared into a cloud of black dust.

It has been suggested that a person should never speak about his fears while in the house. Some of the ghosts do not appear friendly; they will use fear to get someone out of the house. Even some of the regular visitors have witnessed things so frightening that they considered never returning. One such visitor was a man who often volunteered there. He reported that he was alone in the large dining room, when he felt an overwhelming sense of being watched. As he turned and looked toward the door, he saw a soldier, with half of his face burned off, staring at him. The soldier appeared solid and clear, with his arms outstretched. To the volunteer, the ghost looked like a living person, who had just been severely injured. Needless to say, this incident was so shocking that he ran out of the house as quickly as he could. In his haste to vacate the house, he accidently kicked a chair so hard that he broke his foot. Unfortunately, the ghost was not in the line of sight of the infrared camera. The camera did, however, pick up the reaction of the volunteer when he saw the eerie figure.

One of the authors of this book, Bret Oldham, has also witnessed the high strangeness of Octagon Hall. Bret was invited to speak at an event held there to raise money for the museum. In addition to guest speakers, the event included a novice ghost hunt later that evening. Due to the large number of people who showed up for the event, the guests were divided into smaller groups for the novice ghost hunt. Bret was asked to lead one of these groups. His group consisted of 12 people. During the ghost hunt, Bret's group went into the large room on the second floor of the house; this room was used as the sick room during the war. Bret conducted an EVP session in the room, and later analysis revealed several EVPs. It was believed that some of these voices were from Civil War soldiers, still residing in the house.

After the EVP session, the group began to exit the room and move to another area of the house. Billy, the museum curator, and Bret were the last ones in the room. Suddenly, they heard a loud noise coming from the other side of the room. Billy and Bret quickly turned around and looked for the source of the noise. They were shocked to see that the closet door had swung open, and the display case, hanging on the wall beside it, had shifted sideways. They quickly rushed across the room to grab the heavy display case, before it completely fell off the wall and crashed to the floor. Neither man could find a rational explanation for what caused the violent movement of the objects. In fact, Billy knew how difficult that closet door was to open. He asked Bret to shut it and try to open it again. When he did, he noticed that the door was stuck. He had to pull on it, with above normal force, in order to open it. Whatever caused that door to open and move a heavy display case was a very powerful energy.

Perhaps, that particular paranormal incident had something to do with the location of the door. That is the location of one of the secret spots used to hide Confederate soldiers. Maria explained, "There is a secret passageway in that closet that leads to the basement. The theory is that, once they got to the basement, they would take the hidden tunnel in the basement winter kitchen out of the house." Maria continued, "While we were cutting a hole in the wall, that revealed the secret passageway, we had another strange event happen. Everyone was downstairs helping to cut the hole in the wall. One of my team members had placed a camera in one of the upstairs bedrooms. Something grabbed the camera and yanked it, straight up to the ceiling. Later in the day, a lady went upstairs to video, using a handheld camera. We heard commotion coming from upstairs, so I went up there to find out what was happening. She thought that she had filmed a shadow figure, moving around the room in a back and forth motion. After reviewing the video, we could not discern if she filmed a shadow figure or the sun moving back and forth through the clouds. However, as we watched the video and saw her camera try to autofocus on the shadow, we heard a voice on the audio say, 'Get out!' I went back to the room with my K2 meter, and it was going nuts with constant readings. Since that day, we have picked up EVPs telling us how mad "they" are at us for tearing a hole in the wall. We don't know if they think we've defaced the house or that we have exposed one of their hiding spots."

Octagon Hall has secured its rightful place in history. Today, it stands as a painful reminder to a period of deep darkness in the United States. Many lives were lost, and everyone's life was forever changed. The Civil War left deep scars on this country. One can only imagine how strong the emotions and loyalties were of those who lived and experienced it firsthand. Because of these intense emotions, it seems that many of the souls have refused to move on after death. They have lingered, and refuse to surrender. For many of the people who once lived at Octagon Hall or perished there, time stands still. Their ghosts vigilantly remain. For the living, who visit these hallowed walls, the echoes of war still ring.

CHAPTER 9

Heaven's Answer

Life is full of twists and turns. There is an old proverb that says, "If you want to make God laugh, make a plan." Life is also full of unexpected events and surprises. Sometimes these bumps in the journey of life, not only, change our direction in life but completely change who we are as a person. Dying, during a routine surgical procedure, was certainly not something Sasha expected to happen, nor could he have realized how that one event would forever change his entire being. However, both things are exactly what happened, when fate stepped in and greeted him.

Sasha will forever remember October 2, 2014. On this day, he went in the hospital for a minor surgical procedure. At the time, he was working in construction as a solar panel installer in San Diego County, California. It had been a hot summer, and he had put in a lot of hours. During the course of the hard work that summer, he developed a hernia on the left side of his groin which required surgery to repair. When he arrived at the hospital that October day, he thought he would be going home later that afternoon. He knew he would have some down time to heal but looked forward to getting back to work as soon as he was physically able. As it turned out, he did not go home that day. He almost did not go home at all. Something went wrong during the surgery, and Sasha flat lined.

"I have no idea what happened to cause my heart to stop," Sasha said. "My Mom is a laboratory technician, so she knows a bit more about it. She speculated that I was possibly given too much anesthesia which caused my heart to stop. I really have no idea what happened to me. All I remember is being prepared to go under the knife. I was put out. The next thing I knew, I was looking through a tunnel at a bright light. The tunnel had three different shades of darkness to it: black, super black, and not so black, and it was turning and moving around. The tunnel was huge and circular. You could probably fit a diesel semi truck in it. I looked at the light at the end of the tunnel, and it seemed so far away. I said to myself, 'Crap! I have a long way to go.' I decided that I wasn't going to go."

Sasha believes that he was in this tunnel during the time his heart stopped beating. His mother later told him that the doctor had come out of the operating room and told her, "We're sorry, but we lost your son. His heart has stopped." She would not accept that her son had died. She became very upset and adamantly told the doctor to get back in there and bring him back. The doctor agreed to try. To his surprise, Sasha's heart did start beating again. They brought Sasha out of the operating room and wheeled him past his anxious parents. At first, Sasha's mother did not recognize him; he had turned blue and looked very bad. They rushed him to another area of the hospital to continue their efforts to stabilize him. Later, his mother heard two nurses talking. One of the nurses said that Sasha had coded for 37 minutes. His mother, being in the medical field, knew exactly what that meant; he had been dead for 37 minutes. If not for her pleading with the doctor to continue to try and bring him back, Sasha would not be living today.

Eventually, Sasha was taken to a room. He was comatose, but the next day, he opened his eyes. He looked around but did not speak. He tried to remove the wires and tubes from his body and get up. The nurses had to subdue him. He was so adamant about getting out of bed that he had to be strapped down. To protect him from hurting himself, he was heavily sedated. "I don't remember waking up the first time or doing any of that," Sasha said. "It was five days later when I actually woke up and was conscious. I saw the date, and I asked my parents if that date was correct. My mom said 'yes.' I was shocked and confused. I asked my parents what had happened to me. I felt like someone had beaten me with a baseball bat. My chest and the left side of my torso were black and blue. The bruising was a result of the extreme measures the medical staff had taken to revive me and save my life. I was in a lot of pain. I couldn't take a deep breath without hurting, but I was alive." The next day, Sasha had another surgery. There had been damage to his heart from the NDE, so a pacemaker and a defibrillator were placed.

"My mother prayed for me before I had surgery that fateful day. I also prayed which was weird because I'm not a religious person. I don't go to church often, but I do believe in the Heavenly Father and Jesus Christ. I just had a feeling that something was going to happen," Sasha explained. He recalled how he felt while in the tunnel, "The feeling I had when I was in that tunnel and saw the light was incredible. I couldn't curse. I had no negativity in my body. Everything was positive. The worse word I could say was 'crap,' which is not my nature because normally I would have used a curse word. I don't think I was even capable of having any negative thoughts. I wasn't thinking about whether or not I was going to be judged. I wasn't worried about Heaven or Hell. I just felt indescribable, unconditional love. During this event, I must have been aware of what was happening to me because I felt compelled to ask a question. I asked, 'What about the Big Bang Theory?' I didn't hear an actual audible voice, but I heard an answer telepathically. 'That's important but not as important as the point of consciousness,' a male voice replied. I replied back, 'I don't understand.' At that moment, I found myself transported to a bright room with no corners. I was completely engulfed in white light. I was then told, 'The sperm is conscious of the egg, and the egg is conscious of the sperm. Together, they make a higher level of consciousness.' I understood this to mean that they make a being. I was flabbergasted by the profound answers I received. I spoke back to the telepathic voice and exclaimed 'I get it!' At that moment, I woke up, and it was five days later."

This was not the first time that Sasha flirted with death. In 2012, he had a massive heart attack or "widow maker" and had to have an arterial stint. The widow maker is aptly named since few survive it. A few months after his heart attack, Sasha ran into an old classmate who reminded him of an eerie prediction he once made. He related, "About 8 months after I got out of the hospital, I was telling a friend of mine from high school what happened to me, and she started laughing. I asked her what was so funny. She looked at me and said, 'You don't remember do you? When you were 16 years old, you used to tell everyone that you would be dead by the time you were 50.' I had forgotten about that, but the timing of my near death experience was very strange. It happened one month before my 50th birthday."

After he was released from the hospital, Sasha reflected on the lessons he learned from his near death experience. "I had never really thought about pro-life or abortion or anything like that before." He explained. "Now I was realizing that every living thing has consciousness: a leaf, grass, everything that is alive. To me, everything is alive at the point of conception. It starts to have a soul; it's a being at that time. That's how I understood the meaning of what was told to me during my NDE." Sasha continued with his thoughts, "Words can't describe the incredible feeling I had. When I woke up, I was trying to hold on to that feeling for as long as I could; it only lasted a few months. I didn't think that losing that feeling had affected me much, until later. Because of my age and the kind of work I did, I could no longer work with a pacemaker and a defibrillator, so I bought a motorcycle and rode a lot. I would stop at bars, and I began drinking. Over time, my drinking got worse. I would go to a bar four or five times a week. I wasn't drinking beer. I was drinking shots and stuff like that; it got real bad. I had never drunk like that before the NDE incident. About a year ago, I realized what I was doing and knew I had to stop. It was then that I came to the realization that my drinking was because I was depressed. I was depressed because I no longer felt that incredible peace and love that I felt while in the tunnel facing the light."

"I am no longer afraid of dying." Sasha declared. "I know it's not the end. I know that your soul goes somewhere else. What I believed before, I believe even more now, as far as the afterlife goes. The doubts I had before are now completely gone. Even though I no longer fear death, that doesn't mean that I'm going to go out and take chances with my life. It's good to be alive. Even though I have a pacemaker and a defibrillator, I know how lucky I am to, not only, be alive but to have no other damage to my body. After my NDE, the doctors did scans on my heart and my brain. They found a slight abnormality on the right side of my brain. After I regained consciousness on October 7, a nurse gave me some test questions to see how well my brain was functioning. She asked me a series of thirty questions. I got twenty nine of them correct. The one I got wrong was where she asked me to remember five words and then relay them back to her in reverse order, and two of them, I flipped around. To me, it was a miracle to not suffer any brain damage. Now, I go through life with the attitude of whatever happens happens, and how it happens doesn't matter to me. I have no fear now. I feel blessed to still be here. I know that I have been given a second chance. My outlook on life changed after I came back. The dying experience and the answers I received, on the other side, made me look at life differently. It completely changed me and made me a better person. I now realize how fragile and precious life is, not just human life but all life. I don't even kill bugs anymore. Every living thing in our world has a right to live and to share this place; not just me but every living thing.

CHAPTER 10

Soul Travel

Needless to say, when an individual experiences his soul leaving the flesh of its earthy body, it is a profound event, regardless of the circumstances that caused it. This book has discussed the NDE (Near Death Experience) in previous chapters. The OBE (Out Of Body Experience) is the focus of this chapter. Both are characterized by soul travel. The OBE, however, occurs when the soul leaves the body, but the person, having the experience, is not declared clinically dead during the event. These types of incidents also have a profound effect on the experiencer. Due to the parallels between NDEs and OBEs, there are some cases in which it is difficult to ascertain which phenomena occurred. In these cases, it is left up to the individual to determine his own perception of what happened. Such is the case with the accounts in this chapter. Although none had to be revived to return from the other side, the similarities, between their experiences and others who had a NDE, are striking. Did they merely have an OBE under extenuating circumstances, or did they go through a "Near Death Experience?"

Kat was born and raised in Las Vegas, Nevada. Being part Asian and part Caucasian and growing up in the 1960's was difficult for her. Kat also had the ability to see and hear spirits, which caused even further isolation. When she mentioned these abilities, she was told to keep quiet or risk being placed in a mental hospital; she learned that not talking about these kinds of incidents was in her best interest. Because of this, Kat never shared her soul travel experience with anyone, outside her family. This is the first time she has had the courage to reveal what happened to her on that fateful evening in 1995.

"The year was 1995. I was married but have since gotten divorced. I got into an argument with my then husband." Kat recalled. "I went into the bedroom to blow off some steam. All of a sudden, this strange buzzing sound started circling the bed. It kept getting louder and louder; suddenly, I was paralyzed. I could not move my body. I couldn't even scream for help. Then, as if a hand was pushing me up from my spine, my back was lifted up from the bed. I saw large squares of white light beaming down on me. I was terrified!" She exclaimed. "I didn't know what was happening to me. My back was slowly lowered to the bed, and the buzzing sound softened. I also felt that I was able to move again. I jumped out of bed and went to tell my husband what had just happened to me. He looked at me like I had three heads, so I just went back to the bedroom. As I lay back down, I heard the buzzing sound start up again. I quickly jumped up and ran out of the room. I didn't want to risk the same thing happening again."

Kat continued, "About 6 months later, I became very ill. I was getting horrible headaches and was getting nauseous every day. This went on for 3 months. I began to lose my motor skills, and I lost a lot of weight from not being able to eat. The doctors ran every test imaginable on me and could not find out the cause. My blood work showed that my liver enzymes were at a dangerously high level. My doctor told me that I was a walking time bomb, but there was nothing he could do. I was very scared and confused." Kat returned home that day overwhelmed with emotions. She was at her wits end. She decided to lie down and rest to clear her mind, so she could contemplate what to do. As she was lying there, she suddenly felt herself leaving her body. Kat described what happened next. "It's so hard to put into words the feeling I had. It was so peaceful. I was not worried about leaving my son or my family. An unconditional love washed over me; I felt like everything was perfect. I didn't ever want to lose the feeling I had." Kat felt herself return to her body. She felt that she had been given a reprieve from, what she perceived as, death.

"I felt strongly compelled to call my mother one last time." Kat said. "I phoned her to tell her goodbye. I told her that I was not going to make it, and I loved her. She lived close to me, so she rushed over to my place. When my mother arrived, she didn't know what was happening to me; she tried to comfort me by doing reflexology on my feet. In that moment, I felt like I was part in this world and part in the next. After a while, I started to feel like myself again, and I completely came back to my body. That wonderful peaceful feeling started to leave me." Kat continued, "Eventually, my mother was satisfied that I was going to be alright, so she left. Not long after she left, I got very sick to my stomach and vomited for over an hour. I then began to fall asleep, not knowing if I would ever wake up or not. As I was falling asleep, I heard a man's voice in my head say, 'You are a healer and you are going to heal yourself.' At the time, I did not know what that meant."

When she woke the next day, she was still sick but was feeling better. It was then that she decided to take control of her own health. She took a holistic approach, and it worked. She learned the energy healing modality of Reiki. After studying Reiki, her gifts of communicating with the other side and seeing spirits came back to her. Kat reflected back on her strange life changing event, "To this day, I am grateful for that experience and to have a second chance at life. I want to use that experience to help others heal."

David came into this world under very sad circumstances. It seemed that life had dealt him a bad hand right from the start, but, in actuality, he was lucky to even get a chance at life. He was born two months premature in 1970, due to his mother committing suicide. He led a troubled life, mostly due to his mother's suicide. Years later, his older brother followed in his mother's footsteps, and he, too, took his life. It had been hard enough dealing with his mother's death. When his brother killed himself, it was too much for David to bear. He no longer had a desire to live. He purposely overdosed on drugs but failed in his suicide attempt. Instead of dying, he fell into a coma and remained comatose for a week. The doctors informed his family that they did not feel that he would recover, and they should begin to make funeral arrangements for him.

While in the coma, David had what he perceived to be a dream. He recalled the strange experience, "I found myself on a space station with long halls. I looked out a window, and all I saw was deep space. I felt like I had been transported to the future. I was then escorted into another building that looked like an airplane hangar. I was told to go into a conveyor belt type machine and go through it; I obeyed." He continued with his remarkable account, "While in the machine, I had another dream. It was like a dream within a dream. I dreamed about my car, a black mustang. When I reached the other side of the machine, my car was there."

David's experience, while in a coma and waiting at death's door, got even more bizarre. "Then I met a race of people that were very strange. The bodies of the people were contained in vases with their heads sticking out the top. The sides of the vases had tubes coming out, which I was led to believe was for food and waste removal. In this location, gravity was different. It seemed that these strange people, or whoever built this place, could assign gravity in all directions. For us, it would be like having a living room on the ceiling or a wall. I got the idea that it was intentionally done in order to maximize space.

While still in this strange dream like state, David suddenly woke up from his coma. Even though the doctors had given him little chance of living, he fully recovered. A month after being released from the hospital, David felt a strong urge to draw. He had never been interested in art before and showed no artistic talent prior to his strange experience while comatose. "It's like a mission to me now." David said. "I have plenty of inspiration, but it is still very mysterious to me how it happened. The random black and white chaotic scheme I use seems to be a form of writing; although, I'm not really sure. My artwork is a product of my experience. It's very bizarre to say the least!" David is rapidly gaining a worldwide following for his very peculiar style of art.

When one hears the word "soul mate," the image that often comes to mind is that of a lover who has incarnated other lifetimes with you. Although that is often the case, there can be other types of soul mates. They can be friends or family members such as parents, siblings or other relatives. For

Fabiano, that person was his grandmother. He had always been very close to his grandmother and felt a deep connection with her. He felt that they were, indeed, soul mates. When Fabiano was 21 years old, his grandmother died. Her passing left him with an emptiness that he could not fill. She had been the rock that had always been there for him. He was utterly devastated and fell into a deep depression.

Life had not been easy for Fabiano. He was born in the 1970's in Brazil to a single mother who was Roman Catholic. During that time, Brazil was predominately Roman Catholic. Having a child out of wedlock was frowned upon by the church. It was like having a scarlet letter on one's forehead. So, when Fabiano was 18 months old, his mother quickly married his step father to, as he described it, "fix and clean" our family name. Fabiano never knew who his biological father was, thus deepening his need for his grandmother's love.

One night soon after his grandmother's death and while still deeply depressed, he felt himself leaving his body. "My ghost body was wearing the exact same shorts and t-shirt that my lying in bed motionless body was wearing," Fabiano recounted. "I desperately tried to wake my mother and my uncle so they could see two of me, but it was useless. I could not awaken them. I then found myself floating over my house. I could see the entire neighborhood. I felt very cold. Suddenly, I heard a powerful male voice. The voice called me by my first name and said, 'Fabiano, you will head north now. You will speak to Argemiro and then you will speak to Tyler. Argemiro was my step-father. At that time, he was visiting his parents in Paraiba in northeast Brazil. Tyler was a former American Mormon missionary who served in my hometown." Fabiano continued, "Upon hearing this command, I felt something wasn't right. I hated my step-father and did not wish to approach him in any way. Tyler was the first guy that I had fallen in love with; although, I never told him how I felt. Back then no one would even try to understand homosexuality in this country, so I had to hide my feelings."

Fabiano began to get scared. "When the voice mentioned those two people, I began to realize what was going on; I was going to die!" Fabiano exclaimed. "Because of my beliefs, I knew that death would not be the end, but I felt that I was leaving my material body and the material world for good. I panicked because I strongly felt that my mission here was not yet finished. I learned in that very moment that good feelings, like love and empathy, get us attached to people but that bad feelings, like hate, do too. I understood that voice that 'Authority,' would take me to these people to make amends, to break those ties before I left earth. For some reason I felt compelled to recite 'The Lord's Prayer.' I tried but for some unknown reason I could no longer pronounce the words. I tried other prayers; nothing worked! So, I then began to just call out to Jesus. I told him that I was not yet ready to die. This was all happening very quickly." Fabiano explained.

He continued, "I felt like I was quickly being drawn to the sky by a very powerful magnet. All the while, I kept begging Jesus to let me live. I kept repeating that I wasn't ready to go yet. Suddenly, I felt like another magnet was pulling me in the opposite direction back towards my house. I was flying over cities so fast that I could only see a blur of the city lights. My body felt like a rubber band being snapped back. Then I saw my neighborhood and stopped over my house. I went down through the ceiling. I once again could see my physical body still lying on my bed. I couldn't take it. Standing there looking at my body made me very sad. I prayed to God to not let me see this anymore. Then I heard that same voice speak to me again. He said my name and then gave me a number. It was at that moment that everything went black. I woke up in my physical body. I immediately told my mom what had happened. I told her the number that I was given. On her way to work that morning, she played the lottery with that number. Later that day, she came home with extra money that helped us a lot back then. The voice had given me a winning lottery number." Fabiano proclaimed. He believes he was given the winning lottery number for another reason as well. "I feel the number was given to me as another way to verify that my experience wasn't just a dream. It was all real, and that reality not only influenced the spiritual world; it affected the material world too."

Chapter 11

The Lost Children

In the small Kentucky town of Park City sits a once majestic structure best known as the Mentz Hotel. The buildings and its grounds are listed on the national historic register. The original structure was destroyed by fire in the late 1800's. The building, that stands today, was built in the early 1900's. Besides a hotel, the building has been used as a private residence, and from 1946 to 1952, it was the Baulch Junior School for Boys. It also served as a nursing home for several years. During that time, numerous funerals were held on the property. It is also rumored that, at least, two murders happened at The Mentz during its time as a hotel. Currently, it is a Bed & Breakfast.

For many years, locals have reported mysterious happenings in the building. That is not surprising, given the long and colorful history of the property. In recent years, The Mentz has been used as a Halloween attraction. All the reports of high strangeness soon caught the ears of ghost hunting groups, who then began to investigate the place. Not long after the paranormal investigations of the old building began, the evidence of its haunting began to accumulate, and its legend grew. This is how I, Bret Oldham, heard about the property.

I was living in the Nashville, Tennessee area at the time. Some friends of mine, from a local ghost hunting group, scheduled an investigation of the property and invited me to go along. Typically, I am not fond of doing ghost investigations with more than two or three other people, but I was intrigued by the stories that I had heard about The Mentz. So, I accepted their gracious invitation to participate in their paranormal investigation. By the end of the night, I was glad that I did. The ghosts of The Mentz did not disappoint.

It was a warm balmy evening, as I pulled into the driveway and first laid eyes on the old building. It was painted blood red with white trim and had clearly fallen into disrepair. Before I even greeted everyone, I immediately walked to the front of the building and slowly gazed across the façade. I felt a strange sense of eeriness as I gazed up at the widows. Through the dusty glass, I could see traces of the now empty rooms. I had a strong sensation that I was being watched, even though no one was inside at the time. A local woman, who had gotten permission for our group to investigate, was there. She gathered everyone together for a walkthrough of the property. There were ten people on the property that night, eight in the paranormal group and the guide and her husband. As we walked around the property, our guide pointed out some of the more active areas of the hotel and related some of its history. Upon entering, I immediately felt a sense of heaviness. The energy felt thick and dense. There was a coldness to it; it felt sad. Perhaps, the sadness carried over from its days as a nursing home, when the poor souls were waiting on death to call. Maybe, it was from the reported murders that supposedly happened in the building, or it was simply an accumulation of many unfortunate events that took place there. The cause of the negative energy was unclear, but it was intense. I wanted to find the cause of this overwhelming negativity I felt within the walls of this once majestic building.

After the walkthrough was over, I asked the group if it was alright if I went back in for a few minutes. They were all busy getting their equipment ready for the ensuing investigation and did not mind. I took one other person from the group and went back in for a private look around. Being sensitive to energy, I can often pick up areas of a reputed haunted location, just by feeling the energy changes. It was different, however, in The Mentz; the entire place felt active. We scoured the large formal dining room, the grand foyer, and several of the large bedrooms downstairs. We, then, carefully made our way up the broken switchback staircase to explore a bit more of the upstairs area. We passed by a bedroom near the top of the stairs, where it was rumored that a murder took place. If that tragic incident did indeed happen, there was no longer any evidence of it. Walking down the hall going from bedroom to bedroom, it was easy to imagine the many souls that had once slept in the now empty and rundown rooms. As I did, I wondered what fascinating stories these walls could tell if they could speak. I also wondered what the ghosts of The Mentz would have to say now that someone was willing to listen. As we made our way back downstairs to rejoin the group outside, I remarked to my companion that I felt the presence of children in the place. I knew that the building had once been a boarding school for young boys, but I had not heard of any of them dying there. Still, I felt their presence and was anxious to find out why.

We returned to the area outside where the other investigators were. They had finished setting up a main base for the monitoring of the static cams. Everything was ready to begin the investigation. It was decided that we would break up into two smaller groups and then rotate throughout the evening. I stayed outside during the first round and helped monitor the static cams for any activity. Most everyone was carrying some piece of equipment. I have always been, somewhat, "old school" when it comes to ghost investigations. All I use is a digital recorder, a small digital camera, a K2 meter (which picks up electromagnetic frequencies often associated with the presence of a ghost) and, most importantly, my own senses. The static cams were in place, and everyone had their own personal gear ready. It was time to begin the investigation.

The first group spent about 45 minutes in the house. Nothing was picked up by any of them during that time, except for a scream resulting from a prank. I was upset by this. It did not appear that this was going to be a serious investigation. I do not like to waste time on investigations, especially when a location has the kind of energy that this place did. Thankfully, things settled down after that, and the rest of the evening went smoothly. The two groups of investigators began to routinely switch places throughout the evening. One group would monitor the IR cameras from the outside base while the other group would investigate inside, and then they would change positions. As the investigation continued, the ghosts of The Mentz began to make us aware of their presence. The paranormal activity began to accelerate. We started to get unexplainable readings on our K2 meters and some of the other equipment. Since there was no power in the building, this meant that the only thing that would register a K2 reading was either a ghost or a cell phone. Everyone knew that cells phones could trigger the K2s, so appropriate measures to prevent that from happening had been taken.

As the night wore on, so did the ghostly activity. A clear shadow figure was picked up by the static cams in the downstairs hallway. Most of us heard music while standing in the foyer. The volume was low, but it sounded like some type of old instrumental music. We became alarmed as the situation turned physical. "What the Hell?" One of the ladies suddenly exclaimed. She had felt an unseen hand forcibly grab her arm. Obviously, she was shaken by the event but soon gathered herself and carried on. Then, during an EVP session, another female member of the group felt an intense burning sensation on her back. Since there was no power in the building at the time, a flashlight was used to see if we could ascertain the cause of it. We worried that she had possibly been bit by a spider, since she was sitting on the floor at the time. When she pulled down her shirt to see the wound, a shocking anomaly was revealed. She had been severely scratched by something. We knew then that whatever or whoever was in The Mentz did not want us there. The entity seemed to be focusing its attack on the women of our group. Things were getting very interesting to me. I still felt the ghostly presence of children, even though we had yet to find any evidence of them.

The Mentz had not disappointed. We had only been conducting the ghost investigation for a few hours, and we had already collected evidence and personal experiences indicating that the stories of the hauntings were indeed true. The negative energy and the unsettling events had drained everyone, so we all decided to take a break outside. We began to make our way out the side door of the large former dining room. I was the last one in line. As I was about to go through the door, I noticed a very strong hit on the K2 meter that I was carrying. "Check this out," I called out. The two people, ahead of me, turned around to see what was happening. Then, it hit again, peaking the meter. "Bret is getting some strong hits on his K2," they called out to the others. For some reason, I felt strongly compelled to walk back across the dining room and into the entryway foyer in the middle of the building. I walked to that room and stopped in the middle of it. Then, the meter went wild. By this time, most of the others had come back inside, but they stayed against the far wall in the dining room. I yelled out, "Someone get a camera on this!" Another group member quickly entered the foyer and began filming.

I began to use the K2 meter to communicate with the unseen force that was near me. I did not feel threatened at all. Instead, I felt deep sadness. My inner sense told me that it was a child trying to communicate. I explained that I meant the entities no harm and that we could use the K2 meter to communicate; I told them that it would not hurt them. "Come close to the light or simply wave your hand in front of it to make it change colors." I explained. "I want to help you. When I ask you a question, make the lights go off, if the answer is yes." "Do you understand?" I asked. The lights of the K2 meter suddenly peaked. I was encouraged that they understood and were willing to communicate with me. I began my inquiries. "Are you a male?" I asked. The lights lit up. The next question was the one I strongly felt compelled to ask. "Are you a child?" I was not surprised to see the meter once again light up. I continued to try to discern who I was communicating with, and why he was still on the earthly plane. The duration of the exchange was going on well past what normally happens under these circumstances on a ghost investigation; I pulled out my phone, so that it could also be seen on camera. I wanted to prove that it was not my phone causing the K2 meter to activate.

I asked the boy if he was alone in the house and did not get a reply. This meant that there were other ghosts or entities present. "Are there other children here with you?" I asked. The lights went red immediately. I wanted to know how many other children were there, but since this was a yes and no procedure, I could not find out the exact number. I continued with my questions. "Are the other children with you right now?" The answer was yes. "Are there any girls?" Once again, the lights on the meter peaked. I sensed that another ghost was with him. When I asked if one of the girls was with him, he answered yes. The minutes began to pass, as I asked as many questions as I could. It was extremely rare to get this kind of active interaction on a K2 meter for such a long duration. I knew that the children trusted me. I wanted to try and help them if I could. I did not know if they needed help, so I directed my line of questioning to that subject. "Do you need help?" I asked. Almost immediately, the lights on the meter moved. I have been on cases like this before where a more powerful entity or ghost was holding the spirits of children captive, thus preventing them from moving on to where they should be. There are various reasons for this. Sometimes, it is as simple as loneliness in that state of being, or an entity may not want to let go of the power he had over others in his previous life. At other times, it is unadulterated evil.

I asked the children if someone was holding them there. It made me angry when they replied "yes." I was angry at the insidious being, who was holding them there against their desire. At the same time, I felt deep empathy for these innocent souls, whose soul journey was being interrupted by this ghost or entity. I did not know how many children were trapped in that location, but even if it were just the two communicating with me, I knew I had to try to help them. To the dismay of some in the group that night, I began to instruct the children on what they needed to do to move on to the other side. I believed they were stuck because they were afraid of whoever was holding them there. Maybe, it was someone they knew when they were alive, or, perhaps, the entity appeared so strong that it instilled a deep sense of fear in them. Whatever the case, these children were bound to this dimension. I told them they had nothing to be afraid of, and they were being tricked into believing that they could not leave. I asked them to call out to other relatives that they knew were on the other side; these people would help and guide them. I told them to call out to God for protection; I instructed them to look for the light. I told them that, no matter what was keeping them there, it was important for them to go into the light. I tried to encourage them to let go of the tight grip of fear that was holding them prisoner in a dimension to which they did not belong. Soon after that exchange, the communication ceased. The lights of the K2 meter quit moving. I knew that the children had either run out of the energy necessary to activate the lights on the K2, moved away from me, or had followed my direction and successfully crossed into the light. Later that night, I tried once again to contact the children. I did not receive any replies on the K2 meter or on my digital recorder. I like to think that the reason for this is that they did break free from the negative entity holding them and were reunited with loved ones on the other side of the light.

After the incident was over, I saw where I had experienced almost 13 minutes of continued communication through the K2 meter. Even the biggest skeptic would not be able to rationally explain what had just taken place. There was no power in the building that would be a possible cause for the meter to activate. I proved that it was not my phone triggering the lights of the meter. The timing of the responses coincided directly with my questions. Given all this, I and the other witnesses felt that it was indeed intelligent communication from what seemed to be the ghosts of children still present in the building. We were all left with no other possible conclusion. When I rejoined the rest of the group in the adjoining room, I was a bit taken aback to discover that a few were upset that I had tried to assist the children in crossing over and leaving the property. They told me that I should have let them be, so other ghost hunters could enjoy the haunting of the location. I dismissed this idea. I was proud of what I had done and hoped that it was successful. The evidence suggested that there were plenty of other ghosts present anyway.

The rest of the investigation that evening was uneventful. We conducted a "spirit box" session in the entry foyer, where my K2 event took place. As previously explained, a spirit box is simply a radio with the scan button disengaged. The spirits will use the stray frequencies and speak through the white noise of the scan. The technique is called "ITC" which is an acronym for Instrumental Trans Communication. In essence, it is spirit communication through any form of an electronic device—in this case, a radio. The radios that are modified to be used in this manner are often referred to as "spirit boxes" or "ghost boxes." Although ITC is controversial, it is now being seriously looked at by science. I have had some amazing results with the spirit box and have captured some incredible EVPs using them.

The entire group was present for the spirit box session conducted that night. We did receive responses from those who were still residing on the property. However, we did not hear anything from the children, who were communicating with me through the K2 meter. To me, it was a good sign and more validation that they had indeed broken free from the force holding them there and moved on to where they were supposed to be. After the spirit box session was over, we decided to pack up and call it a night. Everyone was pleased with the investigation of The Mentz hotel. We all agreed to get back in touch with each other, once we had analyzed all the film footage, photos, and audio we collected that night.

I was looking forward to seeing the video from the long K2 exchange that had taken place with me. I was also anxious to go over the audio and photos I had taken. Early the next morning, I got to work on my data. I started uploading the photos from my digital camera first, as it is very rare to catch anything on film and usually a quick process. I began looking through the first pictures I had taken upon arrival. I zoomed in and sometimes enhanced a photo in order to see more clearly. I had felt such a strong sense of being watched from the upstairs windows when I took those first pictures that I hoped something might show up peeping down at me from one of them, but, alas, nothing was there. I had also taken some shots during the walk through to use for reference photos. These were taken before the sun had even set and while a couple of the guys were still setting up the IR cameras. I was giving them a quick run though when, all of a sudden, something unusual caught my eye. I saw someone in one of the photos that I knew was not present that night. It was not one of the paranormal group members, and it was definitely not the host or her husband, who opened up the property. It was a child! Needless to say, I was shocked. I could not ascertain if it was male or female, but they appeared to be about

10 to 12 years of age. Given that the figure was wearing pants, I felt like it was probably a boy. There was another person in the picture, but he was easily recognizable as one of the group members. He was busy setting up gear, and from the motion blur, he was moving at the time the photo was snapped. That group member was not even near the ghostly figure. The figure of the child was standing still and looking right at me, although no one saw them at the time. The picture was taken in the largest room of the building, which had once been used as the dining hall. He or she was standing at the far end of the room, and I was standing approximately 35 feet away at the other end of the room when I took the picture.

Ghost of child at The Mentz. © Bret Oldham

Was this one of the children that would later communicate with me through the K2 interchange? Of course, I had no way of knowing. I was now excited to run the audio through my software to listen for any EVPs I might have caught. "Did this child also speak to me audibly that night?" I wondered. I decided to continue to look over the rest of the photos from that night. Nothing else showed up in any of them. However, capturing a ghost on film is extremely rare, and I felt very fortunate to have caught the ghostly image of this curious child. I could not wait to share it with the others. I hoped that one of them had also caught the same image or something else. I emailed the image to the other group members, before I started going over the audio from the investigation. It did not take long for the replies to come back. They all verified that it was not one of us, either in dress, height, or age. They also verified that absolutely no child was present that night. It was a unanimous conclusion; I had caught a ghost on film.

After seeing the ghost of the child in the photo I had taken, I was not in the least bit surprised to find EVPs as I began to analyze the audio. What I was surprised about was the number of different voices I captured. In total, there were fifteen EVPs, and that did not include the spirit box session. I did catch an EVP of a child, but I do not believe it was either of the children that had interacted with me and the K2 meter. This voice sounded like an older male child. The EVP was caught on the front porch of the building, just in front of the main door entrance. It said, "I'm a demon." Although many people would find this alarming, I did not. I saw or experienced nothing that night that would indicate any sort of demonic presence. Actually, in all of the many paranormal investigations that I have been on, I have never encountered anything that I perceived as demonic. I chalked it up as the mischievous actions of a young boy wanting to scare someone. I do feel that there were ghosts on the property, who were angry and filled with negativity but, certainly, not demons.

The most interesting ethereal voice that I recorded during the investigation of the The Mentz Hotel happened while I was on the second floor. I was walking down the main hall with two other members of the paranormal group. One of them was using a ghost hunting device called an "Ovilus." This electronic device will say various words that are supposed to be manipulated by ghosts using electronic frequencies. Personally, I have never been interested in using one, as I have been suspect of the devices validity. On this occasion, the Ovilus had been relatively quiet until, without warning, the robotic voice of the device suddenly says the word "murder." We all stopped and looked at each other. "Did you hear that?" One of the ladies asked. Everyone had heard it. The lady holding the Ovilus checked the history menu and, sure enough, it had said the word murder. It really got our attention, as we were coming upon the room where a murder had reportedly taken place. Was this simply a coincidence that the Ovilus said the word murder near a room where a murder was said to have happened? I caught an EVP right after the Ovilus had said the word "murder." The EVP was from an adult female who bluntly declared, "You can complete that." What an ominous statement from the other side. Negativity did prevail in the old building, and I had just recorded the voice of one of the dark ones. I wondered if she was the one who had held the children there.

I was so impressed by the evidence I had obtained during my investigation of the former Mentz Hotel that a few months later I decided to submit it to the television show, "My Ghost Story." It was not long before I was contacted and asked to appear on the show to which I readily agreed. I was anxious to share the evidence with the world. Besides flying to Los Angeles to film the interview, the producers also wanted to film a segment at the location. The arrangements were made, and we were set to meet at The Mentz that upcoming January. It was bitterly cold the day of the filming. The temperature was only 18 degrees Fahrenheit, not exactly the best conditions to film. The cameraman sent by the production company was not happy to learn that the building did not have power or heat. Two other persons were also there for filming the location segment. One of them had been on the investigation with me and the other was familiar with the property. The filming lasted several hours. I could sense the apprehension building in the cameraman. Eventually, I asked him if he was alright. "This place gives me the creeps," he replied. "Let's hurry up and get this done, so I can get out of here." The ghosts of the old building must have heard him. Not long after his comment, we heard what sounded like some type of movement coming from upstairs. Then suddenly, a door upstairs violently slammed shut! It was almost more than the poor cameraman could take. To me, it was simply a reminder from the many ghosts that haunt the property. Whether they were once guests, patients, residents or students, some of them never left…

CHAPTER 12

Who's That Girl

Although encounters with the afterlife are considered rare, this is certainly not the case. In fact, they are very common, but the subject remains taboo. Most, who do have some type of encounter, only tell a select few about their experience, if they say anything at all. It is rare, however, for several people to encounter the same spirit at different locations. This type of encounter defies the odds, but this is exactly what happened in Fayetteville, Tennessee, a little town near the Alabama border.

As you pass through the quaint little city of Fayetteville, it looks much like thousands of other small towns scattered throughout the south. Tall trees and lush yards dot the streets that are filled with older, well maintained homes that all lead to the historic town square. There is the usual array of fast food restaurants, grocery stores, Wal-Mart, and small shopping plazas. There is nothing that would give the impression of any paranormal happenings there. However, looks can be deceiving, and this is definitely the case in Fayetteville, Tennessee. Reports of Bigfoot sightings, UFOs, and ghosts abound in the area. These reports are not being given by delusional or troubled individuals; they are being told by regular, honest town folk.

Many of the ghost encounter stories come from the old Lincoln County Hospital, which served as the city's hospital for a number of years. Since its closure, it has garnered countless tales of other worldly encounters from those using the building for other functions or from nearby residences. Even the local police have had unexplainable paranormal incidents while investigating possible break-ins and vandalism. However, one of the most intriguing local ghost legends is that of the ghost of a little girl, who has appeared to several Fayetteville residents. What makes this encounter highly unusual is that "the little girl" has appeared to more than one person, and the appearances have happened in different locations and scenarios.

One of the first accounts comes from a local policeman. While out on his tractor one afternoon, he had a serious accident. He was working in a wooded area with uneven terrain when his tractor suddenly lost traction and turned over, pinning the police officer underneath it. He was injured and, due to the weight of the tractor, could not free himself. He had no way to call or seek help, as he was too far from any house for anyone to hear his pleas. Not knowing the full extent of his injuries or what else to do, he laid back on the ground and waited. The minutes seemed like hours, and hope began to fade. He began to entertain the thought that this might be the end for him. He had prayed for help, but no one had come to his rescue. As he was about to give up all hope, he heard the voice of a young girl. He opened his eyes, and through the glimmering sunlight, he saw a child standing near him. She looked to be about five years old and was wearing a blue dress with little pink flowers on it. His first thought was that she was an angel coming to take him to Heaven. Then, she spoke to him. "Don't worry. Everything will be okay." She said. He does not remember if she simply disappeared or just walked out of his line of sight, but he felt a renewed sense of hope and strength after the incident. He held on and was eventually found. He recovered from his injuries and, to this day, is thankful for the mysterious little girl who came to him when he needed it most. It makes little difference whether she was an angel or a ghost. To him, she saved his life, and that is all that matters.

Less than a mile away from where the policeman had his accident, the little girl made her presence known again. A married couple had just moved into their new home on a ridge above the hollow. At the time, they still had no close neighbors. Not long after they moved into the house, they began to experience things they could not explain. Strange smells of perfume began to permeate throughout the house, even though there was no perfume in the home. Cold spots would suddenly pop up out of nowhere. As the house was new, they looked for a logical source for the happenings but could find none. As the weeks passed, the paranormal activity increased in both frequency and intensity. The husband began to hear voices that seemed to be coming from inside the ductwork, and they were especially loud in the master bath area. Once while in the master bath, he heard the voices and noticed that the family dog also appeared to hear them. The dog cocked his head sideways and stared up at the ceiling towards the ductwork. He was quite spooked by the incidents but did not mention them to his wife because he did not want to frighten her. He decided to learn to live with whatever was there, and eventually, they moved.

It was not until many years later that he learned of his wife's experiences with the ghostly inhabitant of their former home. In the midst of a conversation between them about ghosts, his wife revealed that she had witnessed a ghost inside their house. "Did you ever see the little girl in our old house?" She unexpectedly asked him. "I was washing my hair in the kitchen sink and happened to see this little girl out of the corner of my eye standing in the hallway. She was wearing a blue dress with pink flowers on it." She recalled. When she rose up from the sink to get a better look, the little girl had vanished, and she never saw her again.

Remarkably, the restless spirit of the little girl has made even more appearances through the years around Fayetteville. One family, at a newer house in town, recounted seeing her presence. There was a loveseat in the house that she liked, and she was often seen by the family members sitting on the loveseat. She wore, what they described as, an antebellum style dress. She would also go up and down the stairs. At various times, she was seen near the kitchen, silently watching the mother cook dinner in the evenings. It never really bothered the family very much. The young ghost was not malicious and was not trying to harm anyone. Even the kids were not afraid of her. They all learned to live with her occasional manifestations. The problems began when the ghost began to appear to the babysitters. Tales of the haunting spread quickly. It got to the point where the family could not find a babysitter that would work in the house. They decided to call in their priest to exorcise the loveseat where the ghost liked to sit. They never saw her again after the exorcism.

The ghost might have left the house with her favorite loveseat, but she did not leave Fayetteville. It was not long before she made another appearance. She certainly was not shy; her next appearance was at a tea party in front of 44 people. In the January 2011 issue of the online magazine, *Alternate Perceptions*, author Brent Raynes interviewed a lady who gave a firsthand account of this incident of high strangeness with the little girl ghost. He wrote, "In April 2010, I met a charming woman named Peggy, a resident of Fayetteville, Tennessee, who had a fascinating "little girl ghost" type story to share. She lives in a pre-Civil War home and has been having old fashioned tea parties. Peggy began having the tea parties on Good Friday in 2005 with her two granddaughters from Chicago in attendance. Forty-four people were there for the first tea party, which has become an annual event.

'We had mothers, the grandmothers, and the kids,' Peggy told me. 'We all dressed up with hats and long dresses, and the kids all dressed up.' But that first tea party was when the little girl was seen. 'I didn't know the kid, and most of the kids I knew,' Peggy continued. 'She loved the tea. She ordered tea three or four times. She would say, 'We need another pot of tea over here please.' She was probably 7 or 8, but she had a very strong voice; everybody who has talked about it remembers that her voice kind of sounded like an older child.' After the party was over, Peggy realized that no one had signed the register she had provided. Being family and close friends, she began writing down names. I then started calling around. 'Who brought the little girl?' Nobody knew the little girl. After I realized that nobody knew her, I started gathering pictures. Everyone who had taken pictures brought them to Peggy. 'We got all of these pictures together, and there was a place where she was sitting and where she was standing. She didn't show up in any of the pictures.' Peggy stated. Confirmation of the pictures was provided by Mark Kelso, a local respiratory therapist. 'I've seen the pictures. Mark noted. 'You can see where three little girls would be sitting at a picnic table with their glasses of juice and their plates of cookies, and where she would have been sitting in the middle, there is nobody there. The plate is there. The cup is there.'

'She was dressed really cute in a dress that was probably from the 60's,' Peggy explained. 'She had a little red hat and a little white dress with red flowers and red sleeves, and I noticed because she was so cute. We did not see her come there, and we did not see her leave; nobody would have brought a child that age and just dropped them off at a party.' Peggy tried to find out if anyone learned anything about the mystery girl's identity from conversations with her. 'She talked if spoken to,' Peggy said. 'She ordered tea, and my sister took her over to the table and asked her what she wanted to eat, and she kind of pointed to things. We asked the kids if she talked, and one little girl said, 'She would talk to us. She sat at our table, and she ate with us. We asked her name, and she wouldn't tell us her name.''

Do the ghosts of two little girls haunt the small town of Fayetteville, Tennessee, or have all the multiple witnesses encountered the same ghost? The age of the child ghost is most often described as around 5 years old. The witnesses at the tea party thought that she appeared to be closer to 7 or 8 years old. Of course, guessing her age is purely subjective and a matter of opinion. One of the most remarkable aspects of these sightings is that the ghost of the young girl is sometimes seen wearing the same clothing, while at other times is seen in different clothing. It is believed by many paranormal researchers that once someone has crossed over, they can choose to appear in any way they want. They may appear as a younger version of themselves, if they passed as an elderly person. They can also be seen wearing whatever they conjure up in their thoughts. This could provide a rational explanation as to the various clothing the child ghost has been seen wearing. One thing is for sure; the energy needed for a ghost to appear in solid form is immense. For a ghost to appear in solid form for an extended period of time is even greater. This brings up a theory that may seem even more farfetched than the numerous sightings of a ghost. Is it possible that the child is not a ghost at all but rather a traveler crossing through various dimensions? Whether she is a ghost, angel or dimensional traveler, one thing is certain; high strangeness abounds in Fayetteville, Tennessee.

CHAPTER 13

Messages

The veil to the other side is thin. Our loved ones are always closer, much closer than we know. They, at times, will contact us, in their own way. They want to reassure us that they are okay. Sometimes, this is done in a direct manner; a spirit may materialize before loved ones and deliver a message to them. At other times, these messages are communicated to the living in more subtle ways, so they do not frighten the person they are attempting to reach. This chapter contains remarkable accounts of the living receiving messages from their loved ones, who have transitioned. Although often done in different ways and through various means and methods, they all succeeded in giving hope, inspiration and comfort to the receivers.

Adrian grew up in a small town in Mississippi. He had never given much thought about spirit communication and had no belief in the paranormal. That all changed when he was 15 years old. He has never forgotten the events that changed his mind. Adrian recalled how it all began. "I had a friend who lived in Las Vegas. She had terminal cancer and had known about it for awhile." He continued, "Her name was Rachel. At the time, she and I talked frequently through MSN Messenger. We usually had very normal conversations about every day subjects. She enjoyed it as she couldn't get out much because of her illness, so it was a good way for her to communicate. In one of our conversations, I asked her to give me proof of the afterlife after she died. I also asked her if it was possible to bring me something. She laughed at the notion of bringing me something, but she said she would do her best to give me a sign of the afterlife."

"One of our favorite topics was music. We often discussed Beethoven." Adrian recalled. "Well, one night I went to get on the internet. I was looking forward to talking to Rachel. This was a summer night in Mississippi.

It was usually very humid during the summer, but that night, it was unusually dry. As I started up my computer, my step dad and I heard a loud banging on the side door; no one ever uses the front door in Mississippi." Adrian explained. He continued, "The funny thing was that the banging was done with the melody of "Ode to Joy." My step dad and I were both perplexed as to what caused the banging. The sound on the door was loud enough that it didn't just rattle the door; it rattled the shelves inside the house. We ran to the door. When we got there, no one was there. My step dad wasn't worried. He thought it was a dog hitting the door with its tail. He walked back into the house. I decided to stay there and try and figure out what caused the sound. Soon after my step dad walked back into the house, the window, next to me, suddenly fogged up. No other window in the house had this reaction. As I looked at the window, I noticed that it looked like someone had previously drawn something with their finger on the window. I could see the outline of a smiley face."

"Later that same night, I got on Messenger." Adrian remembered. "I saw that Rachel's name was signed on. I was going to tell her what happened. Before I could say hello, I received a message from her screen name; but it wasn't Rachel. It was her sister. She had gotten on Messenger to inform Rachel's friends that Rachel had passed about two hours earlier. That would have been about 30 minutes before everything happened at my house. When I told her sister about what happened at my house, she was not surprised. She informed me that several other friends of Rachel had also received messages from her."

*****

Sometimes people receive messages from the other side on more than one occasion. Such was the case with Suzanne. Her first experience with a deceased loved one was with her maternal grandfather, with whom she had a very close loving relationship. He was diagnosed with lung cancer, and eventually, it spread to his liver. Suzanne recalled an odd conversation she had with her grandfather. "One day, about a year into his diagnosis, I went to visit him on his birthday. I was 19 years old at the time. He was watering his front yard, and I went out to chat with him. As we were talking, he stopped and looked right at me and said, 'By this time next year, everything will be okay.' I thought that it was a very odd thing to say, but a year later, he died two days before his birthday. He was cremated two days later. The night after his passing, I was awakened by the very strong smell of Old Spice cologne. That was my grandfather's favorite cologne. I felt very strongly that he had come to say good-bye to me."

Suzanne also believes that she received a message when her grandmother passed. She too was stricken with cancer. Towards the end of her life, she was at home under hospice care. Suzanne and her family lived near her grandmother. When the hospice nurse felt that the time of her passing was close, she called Suzanne's mother so she could be with her during her final moments. Suzanne recounted the strange events of that night. "When my mother got there, my grandmother looked at her, then looked directly past her, and said, 'Mom!' She continued, "My mother thinks that she saw her mother, my great grandmother, standing there. Upon saying that word, my grandmother took her last breath. This took place around 6:30 AM. Simultaneously, I had a dream where someone was holding a candelabra, and then blew out all the candles. I was awakened from the dream by my mother calling to tell me that my grandmother had passed."

The incidents with her grandparents were not the only time in Suzanne's life that she had encounters with the afterlife. Another amazing event happened with one of her close friends. "I had a good friend named Tania," Suzanne said. "She and I were hairdressers. We were planning on a business venture of opening up our own salon. I always thought that she was perfect in every way: beautiful, smart, funny, and even an excellent hairdresser. Unfortunately, she was extremely insecure. After the birth of her first child at 24 years old, she decided to have breast augmentation and liposuction. I was mortified that she thought she needed to have these procedures, and I wasn't alone in thinking that. After much reassurance from friends and family, she opted to proceed with the surgery. The procedure was a success. While in recovery at the outpatient center, she was experiencing more than the usual amount of pain associated with these two procedures, and the nurse administered more pain meds. She then told her to get dressed. While the nurse was out of the room, Tania stopped breathing. When the nurse returned, Tania was on the floor and unresponsive. When the paramedics arrived, they were able to successfully defibrillate her heart. She was in a coma and remained so for two weeks. During that time, her brain began to swell." It was during this time that something remarkable happened to Suzanne. "One morning I was getting ready for work; I was blow drying my hair. As I was looking in the mirror, I saw Tania behind me. She was peeking around the corner at me, smiling and waving!" I turned around, and she was gone. I called her mother to tell her what I had seen. Her mother told me that me that Tania had just passed away. I know that she came to say good-bye to me."

Suzanne's encounters with the other side did not end with those two incredible incidents. Recently, she experienced a visitation that was a warning, and one that quite possibly saved her boyfriend's life. Her boyfriend, Jack, began to act strangely, so Suzanne started doing Reiki on him. During one Reiki session, she saw the spirit of his ex-wife. She also saw two other spirits that she thought were the ex-wife's sister and mother, and these spirits appeared above them. She was shocked by this visitation but, at the time, thought they were there to comfort him. Suzanne elaborated, "The entire experience with Jack began when I saw a huge molten lava-like glowing orb rising out of the lake behind our house. The very next day, we experienced an isolated macro burst, a severe isolated thunderstorm, here in our town. We lost power for 4 days. It was during that time that Jack began acting strangely. He was unable to remember simple things, called me by his ex-girlfriend's name, and did other strange things. We really didn't know what was going on with him, as otherwise he seemed fine. When the weekend came, I was concerned enough to take him to the hospital. An MRI showed a bleed in his brain. They couldn't see if it was a tumor or not, due to the blood. When it finally dissipated, they saw that he had a cavernous malformation that bled, resulting in a minor stroke." Thankfully, Jack made a full recovery, and his physical side effects were minimal. It seems that the spirit visitation that Suzanne experienced was not meant to comfort Jack but to warn Suzanne of the seriousness of what was happening to him.

*****

The bond between mother and child is a strong one, and one that certainly transcends the death of the physical body. Pamela's mother left her daughter a message that she knew she would understand. Pamela recounted what happened. "In my mother's last days, she constantly held on to a little heart shaped pillow that she had made. Just a few days after she passed, I took it home and placed it with a few others. One day, I came home, and it was moved to another location. I asked my husband, Billy, if he had moved it, and he assured me that he had not. Over the next several days, I would come home and find the little pillow had moved again. One day it just simply stopped. I truly believe that it was my mother letting me know that all was well."

*****

Diana's friend, Sophia, picked a familiar location to send a message. Sophia had died of cancer in her 50's. Diana and Sophia had worked together at the Motorola Company for many years and had remained friends until Sophia's death. Diana used to take her to a monthly acupuncture treatment in Austin, where they both lived. One day, after the passing of her friend, Diana was having an acupuncture treatment and heard a chair creak in the room. It was like someone was sitting in it and then standing up. She then heard light footsteps in the room. Through the window in the room, Diana could see people walking in the hall, but that was not what she was hearing. The footsteps were coming from inside the room where she was receiving treatment. She felt it was her friend letting her know that she was okay on the other side, so she called out to her by name. She told Sophia that she knew it was her and that she missed her. As she did, the footsteps suddenly stopped.

*****

Departed souls often show up in our dreams. This may be caused by grief and a longing to see the person again, or we may dream of loved ones after thinking or talking about them. In addition, these visitation dreams are easily distinguishable from other dreams, for they bring a message from our loved one on the other side. Firelei has gotten signs through dreams, and she recalled one such occasion. "Back in 2014, I dreamed of my great uncle." She said. "He passed back in 2003. We weren't very close, but in the dream, he insisted I talk to his wife, my great aunt. The next day, I had the same exact dream, so I messaged my aunt Angela, their daughter. There was a third dream two days later, but when he tried to tell me the message, there was static; I couldn't hear him. It was like he wasn't allowed to tell me the message. Even though my aunt was very skeptical, I told her about all the dreams." Firelei continued, "Days later, my great aunt fainted, and a few weeks later, tests revealed that she had cancer. On November 11, 2014, I was checking my Facebook page on my phone, and suddenly, my phone went crazy. The app closed, and the screen started typing by itself the number one. It did it repeatedly all over the screen. I yelled for my Mom, and she came into the room. She then told me that she had just heard that my great aunt had passed away. At that moment, my phone went back to normal." Firelei received one more message from her great aunt in a dream. "I don't eat meat, but last Christmas I had a dream about my great aunt. She was telling me to bake the turkey with rosemary. I told my aunt Angela about the dream. She said that for the first time she used rosemary to season the turkey. I told her that it was validation that my great aunt was communicating with us.

*****

Children are often more in tune with the other side than adults. Their senses have not yet been obscured by the constraints of the dogmatic beliefs of society. While many children have imaginary play friends, some see things that are not imaginary. Stacey found this to be true after a heartwarming incident happened with her granddaughter. "My granddaughter Savannah was at my house one day, looking out the window. She asked me who the man was in the back yard. I looked, and there was no one there." I said,

'Savannah, there is no one there.' She said, 'right there Zsa-Zsa, her name for me, and pointed with her finger where the man was walking. She then said you know him. She got up and walked to a picture of my Dad, who had passed away three years before. She was only one when he passed, so she didn't know him. I felt happy knowing that he was still around…."

*****

Do characteristics of our personality carry on when we leave this physical plane of existence? Of course, they do. That even pertains to our sense of humor, as was evident in this account. Chandra's father was only 51 when he suffered a sudden and fatal heart attack. He was making plans and living life when he died. He had just had his first grandchild, who was just 10 months old at the time of his passing. Since then, he has made his presence known to his family several times.

"My father was a prankster in life and loved to scare the crap out of us all the time. He hasn't changed." Chandra stated. "My first physical encounter with him happened while I was sitting at the computer. I suddenly felt someone grab my chair and shake it hard!" She exclaimed. "It startled me for a moment, but I knew it was Daddy, and typical of him at that." "If something has gone on with one of the family that he doesn't like, he will pound on the brick hearth. You can hear a distinct sound of flesh hitting the brick." Chandra recalled other funny pranks that her Dad has pulled. "He loves to mess with my brother-in-law when he's in the shower. The bathroom door will open and close, and the toilet lid will slam down. On the way to the cemetery after his funeral, the hearse got a flat tire. My nephew was sleeping in the limo during the procession. He started smiling in his sleep, at the exact time the hearse got the flat tire. The family has always laughed about it and joked that my Dad must have whispered in my nephew's ear when it happened. Daddy would have laughed about it!"

*****

Throughout Laura's life, she has heard the voice of what she perceived to be a guardian angel or spirit. This male voice could be heard in a very clear manner and usually came with words of encouragement or warnings, but this was not the only warning that Laura has received from the other side.

In 2001, just four days after 9-11, Laura's sister was reportedly murdered by her husband. Others argued that she killed herself. Since her untimely death, she has visited and guided Laura from the other side. One event happened on a trip to Alaska. Laura vividly remembered, "I had fallen asleep on the passenger side of the car. When I woke up, I felt like I was in two different dimensions. I looked up at the clouds, and I could see my sister's face in them. There was a man standing behind her. My hand reached out to touch her. She looked frightened and mouthed the words 'turn around' to me. Then, the side of her head blew away, and I was brought back to reality. I did not know it then, but my sister had been shot in the head."

In 2002, Laura's life took a drastic turn for the worse. She had been happily married for five years. Her husband was a recovering meth addict but had stayed clean since before their marriage. One day, he called Laura at work and told her that he had the drugs again. She begged him not to take it. He told her that he was going to take it with or without her, so she quickly left work to meet him. That day, she made a fateful decision to join him and soon fell into a downward spiral of drug abuse. Four months later, she walked out on her job. After several more months of living in the grip of drugs, she had a very strange dream. In the dream, she was back in what seemed to be medieval times. She saw many strange characters in the dream that she could not understand. When she awakened the next morning, she woke up with her first migraine.

Soon after that night, she began to hear warnings from the other side. Laura explained, "I would hear things like, 'I don't want to watch you die' or 'this is not the life I chose for you.' This was also the time my sister Irene, who had died a year earlier, would appear to me. At first, she was very elusive. One morning, I followed her down the street but could never catch up to her. Then she began to confront me about stopping the drugs and telling me that I was going to die." Laura continued, "During that time, other people, who had died, would come to me. I was asked if I wanted to 'go home.' I could hear them arguing about it. Some said that I needed to go home because of the extreme emotional pain I was in at the time. Someone else, who was angry over what was happening to me, ignored their pleas. One time I heard him yell, 'when she dies, you die," and at that moment, a huge surge of energy went through the house and tripped all the breakers. It then became very still and quiet in the house."

One night after that incident as I was falling asleep, I heard a voice calling out to me, 'Laura, Laura, where are you? I can't find you.' I opened my eyes and looked around the room, but no one was there. The voice spoke again, 'there you are! I got you into this, and I will get you out!' He exclaimed. "They" began fighting for my life, but I certainly did not know why." My life was surrounded by drugs, criminals, and abuse. My spirit friends convinced me to call my family for help. My Mom sent me a bus ticket, and I left. I never looked back. I spent the next two years healing with the help of my family and the encouragement from my guardian spirit. I used to fear the communication I would receive from the spirit world, but now I have embraced it, and life is good."

*****

Our deceased loved ones have a knowing that we do not have, while living in this fleshly realm. Death of the physical body cannot and will not break the deep emotional connection of love. Once that bond is made, it is eternal. Our thoughts are energy. When we miss and think about someone, who has crossed over, those thoughts are released as energy. The person, on the other side, can pick up that energy. If the emotions, behind the thoughts, are strong enough, the loved one can come to comfort the living. We believe that this is indeed what recently happened to us, the authors of this book.

Julie and her brother Jason always had a loving relationship with their grandparents. Visiting their home in rural Alabama was always a joyous occasion for them as they were growing up. They would go every summer and spend a week with them. During these visits, they would go swimming, walk nature trails, and visit other relatives. As Julie said, "these moments were some of the best of our lives." In March 2005, Julie's grandfather fell and broke his hip. A few weeks later, he died from complications of pneumonia. After his passing, her grandmother was cared for by her mother and aunt. In April 2007, while under hospice care for bladder cancer, Julie's grandmother died peacefully at home. Although she mourned the loss of her grandfather, it was very difficult for her to let go when her grandmother passed two years later. She still has photos of them displayed in her house and often talks about all the wonderful times they shared together.

These memories were stirred in March of 2018, when Jason visited the old family home. No one had lived in the house since the elderly couple, and time had taken its toll on it. Jason took pictures of the outside of the house and of the old, now decrepit barn out back. He shared the pictures with Julie and their parents. It was difficult for Julie to see the condition of the property. The pictures also brought back a flood of good memories. She began reminiscing to me about her grandparents and telling me several times how much she missed her grandmother. Then, she was visited by her grandmother in a dream. I told Julie that her grandmother must have sensed her sadness, and that was why she came to visit her in a dream. She wanted Julie to know that she was still with her and still loved her. The dream helped, but Julie was still feeling that sense of loss that all of us have felt at some time in our life.

A few days after Julie's grandmother appeared to her in a dream, something remarkable happened. Julie and I were sitting on the couch in her den. It was quiet in the house. Julie was lying on the couch to my left, with her back propped up on some cushions. I was sitting facing forward. We were talking, and suddenly, I noticed a figure peep around the door frame, directly behind Julie. "What's the matter?" Julie asked as she saw the surprised look on my face. "I just saw a woman step out from the corner of the door frame!" I exclaimed. Thinking that someone might have broken into the house, we both jumped up to look around the house. We found no trace of anything suspicious. The doors and windows were secure. "Even though she appeared as solid as us, it must have been a spirit." I proclaimed. Julie has lived in the house for several years without any kind of paranormal activity and I had never sensed or witnessed anything unusual in the house before, but it was the only explanation I could find.

Julie asked me to describe the woman to her. "She had short dark hair and was wearing a long sleeve brown colored blouse." I answered. "How old and how tall was she?" Julie asked. "She was maybe in her mid to late 30's." I replied. "I'm not sure how tall she was." I showed Julie where the woman was in the door frame, how she peeked around, and then quickly stepped back. I asked Julie to reenact the movements of the woman; I sat back in the same position on the couch, where I had been a few minutes earlier. As she did, I jumped up. "Oh my God!" I shouted. "Her profile looked just like yours." I asked Julie to stand by the door frame, so I could check her height in relation to the height of the woman. From that, I ascertained that the woman was a bit shorter than Julie. Julie then left the room and came back with a photo. "Did the woman look like her?" She asked as she pointed to a middle aged woman in the photo. "I only got a brief look at her face, as she looked down at us. It was mostly her profile that I saw, but yes, it did look like her." I replied. "This is my grandmother when she was younger. My profile is very similar to hers." Julie said. "It was her." I said. "She knew you were missing her and thinking about her a lot, so she came." I told Julie that her grandmother knew that the dream was not enough to comfort her, so she appeared that night. Since I have had more experience with spirits, they no longer scare me. This was why she let me see her and not Julie; she did not want to scare her.

Julie was elated that her grandmother would make that kind of effort to show her enduring love. I was happy to be the intermediary and deliverer of the message. Julie expounded, "When Bret said my grandmother was "peeking around the corner," this was not out of character for her at all. I can remember times when she did this to check on us or to see what people were doing." That was exactly what she did that night. It was like she was simply looking in on us to see if Julie was alright. At the same time, she was letting us know that she was alright too. Then Julie told me something that that made us further understand the significance of the visitation. "I think I know why grandmother chose today to visit." Julie explained. "Today is her birthday."

Two months later, Julie was celebrating her birthday at her parent's house. Julie described the experience. "We were sitting on the sofa eating birthday cake. Suddenly, Bret had a strange look come over him. I asked him what was wrong, and he said he would tell me later. 'It's my grandmother, isn't it?' I inquired. He said, 'yes.' I could not wait to hear what had occurred. As we were driving home, he told me that my grandmother was indeed there, and she was very happy. He said she continued to say how happy she was and how much she loved me. She also said, 'make sure you tell Julie.' Needless to say, I was elated. It made my birthday even more special."

*****

Everything happens for a reason. I am sure you have heard this expression at some point in your life, and most of us believe in the truth of this statement. Although we may not realize or clearly see the reason some things happen, we usually eventually understand. The death process can be a time when we find ourselves questioning the reason and asking "why?" It takes time to understand why some souls are not on this plane of existence anymore. Perhaps, this is one of the reasons that the departed send messages to their loved ones. We find comfort in these messages, knowing that they are happy and are still with us in spirit. We find comfort in learning with a degree of certainty that death of the physical body is not the end of our existence, but simply a new beginning. In this next story, we see both sides of the spectrum.

Vicki grew up in Kentucky and is now a prominent figure in the entertainment business. She has always been a spiritual woman with a strong faith in God. Like so many others, there have been times in Vicki's life that she has received messages from those who have crossed over. She has also been used as a messenger for those who, unbeknownst to her, were about to cross over. Vicki explained, "Several times in my life I've had situations where I would be introduced to someone about six months to a year and a half before they died. The odd thing was that they always brought up discussions about heaven and God, picking my brain about my personal beliefs. They would ask me things like where something in the Bible was located or what my beliefs were based upon. I would end up being close to them for a period of time. We would go to lunch, and they would ask these types of questions. These weren't people that I would normally hang around; it was like our paths were meant to cross. Then, we would separate. Sometime later, I would have a flash that they were going to die, and I would usually know how they were going to die. At the time, I didn't really understand the meaning of what I was seeing. After their deaths, I would attend their funeral. Inevitably, someone would come up and tell me that they remembered the deceased person saying I had helped them by telling them about heaven and what happens we pass."

"After awhile, I began to feel like the angel of death. When people would come into my life and start talking about these kinds of things, I knew that that person was not long for this life." Vicki continued, "So about ten years ago, I prayed and asked God to take me out of this role. It had gone on for so long. This had started when I was in third grade and had been going on for decades. After I prayed and asked for it to stop, it did stop. After about five or six years, I finally came to peace with it. I understood the solace I was providing people to be able to move forward and to be prepared for what was to come. If that's the way I am to be used, then I am now okay with that. It continues to this day. I now have learned to recognize it. Often, I will be led to people, like meeting them at a new job or in some unusual manner. After they start asking the same questions, I know the reason why our paths crossed."

The people that Vicki meets, who begin to ask her questions about the afterlife, are not always strangers. She had a boyfriend in high school named Steve. Many of their conversations were about the same subject. "Steve didn't really understand heaven. His religious upbringing had taught him to fear God." Vicki remembered, "We had talked about it many times. Eventually, he felt that he had gotten a better understanding of my beliefs about God and the afterlife. Later on, he broke up with me. She continued, "About a year later, we were both in college. I began to have these dreams about needing to call Steve. I felt strongly compelled to call him, but being a female, I would never call a guy first at that time. I wrestled with it for three weeks, but it wouldn't leave me. One night while I was sleeping, I sleepwalked. I had never sleepwalked in my life. I lived in a sorority house, and the phone was in the hall. I got up, went to the phone, and I called him. I hadn't talked to him in over a year. It was two or three in the morning, but he answered. I said, 'We need to talk. When can we talk?' He told me that he would come by tomorrow. I said 'okay,' hung up the phone, and went back to bed. I didn't remember doing any of it. I know it happened because there was a girl, who was up late working on a project, that saw and heard everything."

Vicki met Steve the next evening. "I was downstairs working phone duty, and Steve came in. 'What are you doing here?' I asked. He said, 'You called me last night.' 'I did not.' I replied. We argued a bit about whether or not I had called him. He told me that I had asked him to come talk to me, and that was why he had come. I told him that it wasn't a good time. We agreed to meet the next day. I went up stairs and asked the girls if I had been talking on the phone the previous night. That's when I found out that I had been. The next night, Steve came by. In all, he came to visit me for the next three nights. Each night, we sat for hours in his car and talked about the same subject of what happens when we die, heaven, hell, God, and so on." Vicki recalled some strange things Steve told her. "He told me that he was having dreams that he was going to a place, where no one would be coming with him. I asked if he meant like getting on a bus or something like that. He didn't know but felt he would be going by himself. I told him the dream didn't make sense. Then he said that he didn't feel like he was ever going to get married. He said something was coming, but he didn't know what; yet he seemed to know that he was getting ready to move on."

Vicki continued, "I had longed to get back together with him. That was my focus, so I didn't realize what was happening at the time. It was the week before New Year's Eve. I already had plans for the night, so we agreed to talk again right after New Year's Day. He told me that he that he was going to be taking a trip. 'What do you mean you're going to be taking a trip?' I asked him. 'I don't know where I'm going. I just know that I'm going to be taking a trip.' He replied. He wasn't making any sense. Later, I would understand." Vicki sadly recalled what happened on that New Year's Eve. "Steve was out that night with a bunch of friends, that we both knew. Someone had set me up on a blind date that night. If I had not already had plans, I would have been in that car with them. At around 8:30 that evening, I got up from dinner and went to the restroom with one of my sorority sisters, who was with us. When we got in the restroom, I looked at my watch and said to her, 'I wonder what Steve is doing right now?' It turned out to be the exact time that Steve was killed in a car accident. I didn't find out about Steve until after midnight when I got home. It was then that I found out the time of the accident."

Years after Steve's passing, Vicki felt that he was still letting her know that he was with her. It was usually during low points in her life when she was feeling sad or depressed about not having a special someone in her life. She explained, "Steve's favorite band was the group Foreigner, and his favorite songs were 'I've Been Waiting for a Girl Like You' and 'Cold as Ice.' Every time I went through one of these bouts of sadness and loneliness, one of those two songs would come on the radio. I would then feel an overwhelming feeling of love like Steve was saying, 'Just remember that I felt that for you when I was here. I'm still here for you. You are never alone.' There was no mistaking the timing of these songs coming on the radio, right at the time I needed it. I knew he was there. He knew how to communicate with me in a way that I would recognize." Strangely enough, Steve used to honk as he passed Vicki's house on a nearby multilane road. The spot, where he would honk his horn, was the exact spot where the accident happened that took his life.

A few years ago, Vicki attended a spirit box session that one of the authors of this book, Bret Oldham, was conducting. She had been invited by a mutual friend. Vicki had never participated in a spirit box session before and really did not know what to expect. She had simply come there out of curiosity and to observe. There were eight or nine people in attendance that night. During the session, Bret asked the others to speak up if they heard a familiar voice or heard a name that had meaning to them. He asked the spirits if there was anyone on the other side who had a message for anyone present at the session. Everyone heard a quick and clear reply of "Yes." Then Bret asked who was speaking. We heard a male voice answer, "Steve." Vicki immediately spoke up. "Did anyone else hear the name "Steve" just then?" She asked the group. Every single person there also heard it. Vicki felt that Steve had used this method of contact so that she could hear his voice once again and know that he was okay. From the messages received that night, she felt that it was his way of thanking her for all the long talks they had had which had erased his fear of death and prepared him for his transition. It seemed to give them both peace.

There have been several times during Vicki's life where she was the one preparing someone else for the afterlife. Sometimes she knew it; at other times, she did not. Then, there was the time when someone, on the other side, gave her a message that saved her life, and she was aware enough to listen. "I was working at a CBS affiliate in Dallas," Vickie recalled. "The news team had decided to do something called "Salute Texas." They were taking their news team out all over the state of Texas for three weeks including: San Antonio, Guadalupe Mountains, Austin, and other areas. I was one of two people who flew ahead to these locations to do some promos and marketing. I would send stuff back to Dallas, so it could air. The very first place we were going was the Guadalupe Mountains. We had to get special permission to fly a helicopter to the Guadalupe Mountains because there had been so many accidents there. In fact, the Governor had to approve our pilot to fly in there. This pilot had trained other pilots in the Swiss Alps, so he understood that type of wind shear. We flew up to the Guadalupe Mountains for the very first broadcast. We had thirteen news vehicles, a satellite truck, and the helicopter. It was a pretty big deal."

Vicki continued, "I had gone up in the helicopter to take some aerial footage prior to the broadcast. When I initially put my hand on the helicopter to get in, I saw a flash in my mind of two men out in front of the helicopter lying on the ground. The whole helicopter was shattered. The men were dead. I couldn't see who they were. I just saw two men. I didn't see a woman in my vision. I knew that there were going to be three of us in the helicopter. I didn't think it had anything to do with us, and I got in. We went up and shot all the footage we needed. We came back down, and the pilot remarked that there was a light showing up on the controls. He remarked that he needed to check it out. He asked if we wanted to go up again, after he got back, and shoot more video. He explained that he had to go down to pick up food for everybody, and we could do it then. I said, 'Great! We'll meet you back here.' When the time came that we had agreed on, I got up to go meet them. Suddenly, I felt two hands on my shoulders, but no one was around me. Then I heard a voice telling me, 'You're not going anywhere. You're staying here.' I didn't understand why I was hearing this or why I felt these heavy hands on my shoulders. The videographer came up to me and told me to hurry up because we had to go. 'We're not going.' I told him. 'Why?' He asked. I couldn't give him a good answer. 'I don't know.' I replied. 'We're just not going.' He said okay and that was that. We knew that, when we didn't show up, they would go ahead and take off without us to go get the food."

The helicopter that Vicki and her videographer were supposed to meet did take off without them. It flew on down to Van Horn. During that time, the newscast aired. Vicki remembered the time, "They were getting ready to wrap up the newscast, as it was about 6:25, and it ended at 6:30. The helicopter was coming back at the time, and, suddenly, it fell from the sky and crashed. My videographer and I rushed to the crash site. He couldn't walk up to it because it looked so bad. I walked up, and I saw the exact scene from my vision. The two men were lying in front of the helicopter, and they were both dead. After all the ensuing chaos had ended, my videographer came up to me and said, 'I don't know how you knew, but thank you for saving my life.'"

*****

Mary's father passed away in 1999. Her mother remarried a year later in 2000. Almost a year to the day of his death, Mary's father came to her in a dream. He wanted her assistance in delivering a message to her mother. Mary vividly remembered that dream, "In the dream, my father picked up a pen and paper, but the pen would not write. He commented that he forgot that things did not work the same for him since he left. He told me that he would have to tell her another way. He asked me if I would help him, and, of course, I said I would. He stated that there was a big trunk at my mom's house and inside it was a note. He then folded his paper to show me how it looked. He told me to tell her to read the letter, and he meant everything in the note twice as much as the day he wrote it. He told me that he loved me. He then proceeded to walk into his bedroom and look inside a chest of drawers for underwear. He said he was going to take a bubble bath, which I thought was very weird."

Mary related what happened next. "Upon awakening, I called my mother to tell her about the strange dream. She first explained that my dad loved to take bubble baths and did so at least once a week. She then told me that she had cleaned out the trunk when she remarried and had organized it. She was sure that there could be nothing left in there from my dad. She called me about two hours later, and she was crying. Apparently, curiosity had gotten the best of her. She said that she opened the trunk and found a note sticking up between some papers. It was folded just as I had described. She opened it and read the letter that my father had written to her in 1960 after an argument they had had. It stated that it seemed like yesterday that she bore him a son, like last week since they married, and like last month since their first kiss. He asked for forgiveness for all he had ever done wrong. At the end, it read, "Even as my hands are folded in death, I will continue to love you with all my heart."

CHAPTER 14

A Gift Enhanced

Angela Ashton is a psychic detective for law enforcement who primarily works on search and rescue cases, missing person cases, and cold case files. Although her mother told her that she believed Angela exhibited psychic abilities as a toddler, those gifts were greatly enhanced when Angela had a near death experience at the tender age of two years old. The life altering event happened during an emergency appendectomy surgery when her body temperature spiked to 108 degrees. Although she vividly remembers what she saw during the NDE, she does not remember ever telling her parents about it. If she did tell them, they never brought it up to her.

Angela recalled her incredible experience. "I remember feeling as though I was floating, floating away from myself. Suddenly, I was above the room looking down at myself, the doctors, and the nurses. They were in a panic, pumping on my chest. I heard someone say, 'Hurry! She is flat lining.' Then suddenly, it was as though I was being sucked into a tunnel backwards at a rapid speed. When I came out of the tunnel, a feeling of peace and warmth overwhelmed me. Everything was just so beautiful and bright and peaceful. I saw colors I had never seen before." She explained. "There were beings walking around, but they were just emitting light. It is hard to describe these beings. They were shaped like people but with no hair. They were made up of a bright white light, that we don't have here. There was nothing physical about them. Seeing this light was like looking directly into the sun on a bright sunny day, only it doesn't blind you."

Angela continued, "The beings weren't exactly like humans but almost like a mix of human and alien. Their bodies were thin with larger heads and long slender fingers. They had no faces. They spoke to me using telepathy. One of them came and took my hand and took me for a stroll. We communicated telepathically. He told me that our reality is not what we think it is. He said that I would be helping and teaching. He explained to me that I had to go back because my contract was not finished. He told me that big things would happen in this lifetime, and I would be helping others during one of the most important times in history. I can't remember exactly how he worded it, but he made it sound as if I had been here many times before with different missions. I say "he" because it sounded like a male voice to me in my mind. He said that I was different than the others and called me an "ancient." Then, he walked me to the tunnel and told me goodbye; I went backwards through the tunnel." The next thing Angela remembered was once again floating above her physical body. "I could hear the doctors and nurses saying, 'She has a pulse. She's breathing.' Suddenly, I was back in my body and awake. I looked over to this metal tray, and there was this long thing in there that looked like pink chewing gum with teeth marks down it. I guess that was my appendix! I don't remember anything else until I was being bathed in a little yellow plastic tub at a sink."

Even though Angela's NDE happened at such a young age, it still changed her perception of the world. She grew up questioning religion. She said, "I don't put much faith in the Bible. I believe it is a book of stories and rules written by men to control society. I believe religion is man-made to conquer and divide. I do think God is the Father and the "sun." God is light. I believe the sun creates life, and we are all part of it. I'm extremely spiritual, but my views are far from the norm. I think the earth, sun, stars, galaxies and constellations are all spiritual in nature."

Like so many others who have gone through a near death experience, Angela has psychic gifts. "I already had psychic gifts that my mother spoke of before my NDE, but I believe the NDE experience heightened everything to the maximum potential. These psychic abilities have led me to the work that I do as a psychic detective for law enforcement and search and rescue on missing person's cases." Angela continued, "I can read photos, auras and people. I don't like labels and don't really know all the labels, so I would have to google it to name all my psychic gifts. I used to use telepathy a lot when I was a child. I also used psychokinesis a lot. Around the age of 13, my mom told me to stop doing all those things because it was scaring people. She always came to me for advice and paid close attention to any dreams or warnings I gave. She trusted my abilities but never spoke of it or any of the strange paranormal things that seemed to follow me all through life." Angela gave some examples of her psychic abilities, "As a child I loved going on road trips. As we drove past houses and land, I could see history playing out like a video in my mind. It would all happen very fast. I still do it. I can walk into a house and see bits and pieces of everyone that ever lived there in video form. It's the same with land. I often see Native Americans on the land."

Angela elaborated further on her psychic gifts. "It's almost like having two brains, and one of them absorbs information at the speed of light." She said. "I have a "knowing" of things. I can't describe it. I have a wealth of information; yet, I don't know where it comes from. I can be in a group conversation and a person will mention something that I have never heard of, and I will know all about it. This is especially strong with ancient civilizations, artifacts, astronomy, biology, and health/medical terminology. It's like the information has always been in my mind, even though I have not encountered it in this life time."

The views and perception of death are often changed for those who have stood on its doorstep. Angela is no exception. "There is nothing to fear." We do live on. Energy never dies; it only changes form over and over again. Death is only a transition to the next form. The belief that we are reunited with loved ones is only partially true. I believe that loved ones, who have not moved on to their next form, can meet you at the entrance, but most have moved on to their next assignment, for lack of a better word. I don't know that this is a reality that most can accept though, so it's not something I usually tell people. Angela continued, "I believe that we are all connected, not by creation but by reincarnation…. It's a soul thing. We have all been reincarnating since the beginning of time. That is all; we are all connected. This place that I went to during my NDE is a place where souls can rest, so many do not immediately reincarnate. The old souls choose to reincarnate immediately over and over and have much wisdom. Others choose to rest. There is one more important thing. I don't believe in Hell, at least not in the traditional sense as we are taught by religion. It's all in the mind. There is nothing to fear about that either."

CHAPTER 15

A New Direction

Life has its ups and downs. At one time or another, all of us have asked the age-old question—what is the meaning of life? We also may wonder what our purpose is? Some people never find out because they do not pay attention to the signs from the universe. The universe, source, or God, however you want to refer to it, has a unique way of guiding us, if we simply become aware of it. When things are not going right in life, that is a sign to do to something differently. When things are going well, and you are meeting little resistance; you are on the right path. When you refuse to pay attention, the universe will often resort to extreme measures to guide you to where you are supposed to be. For the woman in this chapter, the universe went to extremes to communicate, but that was necessary to lead her in the new direction that she was destined to go.

Lee Papa is an internationally known wellness speaker, mindfulness meditation trainer, and author of *The Temple of All Knowing*. It was a long, arduous journey that led Lee to where she is today. That journey culminated in a near death experience that changed everything. Lee discussed how it all began, "I was in a space in my life that was less than optimal. I was always sick. This had been a trend throughout my life. I grew up with a lot of drama in my house. I was used to having chaos in my life, so when I grew up, I created a world with lots of chaos, drama, and illness in my life. I had to control everything."

Lee continued with her account of what lead to her near-death experience. "Things in my home life were not going well. My husband was in a bad car accident and living with pain from his injuries. My mother was living with us, and that was causing a strain on everyone. My son was small, so I was taking care of him too. On top of all that, we were having financial difficulties. It was all putting an unbearable strain on my marriage and on me personally. I was looking for ways to handle, heal, and fix the situation." Lee recalled how it eventually affected her health. "I had gotten an upper respiratory infection, which was not uncommon for me. My husband had decided to go on a retreat where he would be practicing 'noble silence,' which meant he did not speak for the ten days of the retreat. Obviously, this also included no telephones. He would hand over his cell phone and refrain from speaking the entire ten days of the retreat. So, we knew that we wouldn't speak to each other for those ten days."

"About a week prior to him leaving, I got an upper respiratory infection which I was trying to cure using holistic methods, but I wasn't getting better. I was still working and going about my day as usual. Every day I was feeling more and more depleted. Before he left, my husband insisted that I go to the doctor and get some antibiotics. He said that he would feel more comfortable leaving me, if I was taking antibiotics. So, I went to the doctor, and he prescribed antibiotics. After a couple of days, I wasn't getting better. In fact, I was getting worse. By Sunday, I found myself desperately ill in bed, and my three-year old son was running around the house unattended. My mother was living with us, but I couldn't find her to help. I was so weak, but I did manage to get to the phone and call the doctor. I could only whisper. I told him that I wasn't better, and I was getting worse. They called in another prescription for me, but I was never able to pick it up. I was so worried about my son. I managed to call a good friend of mine who happened to live just a few streets away. I told her about my illness. I asked her to come to the house, pick up my son, and keep him over night, which she did. I don't even know how I got the strength to get out of bed, but I did. I don't even remember if I said anything to her when she arrived."

After her son left the house, Lee got back into bed. At that point, she felt that she could not continue to struggle. She was very weak and tired. She knew her son was safe. It was then that she felt like letting go. Lee recalled what happened next. "I was released. My spirit left my body. The only way I can describe it is like a roller coaster ride. You're going up and going down, and it is thrilling. When the ride is over, however, you don't want to do it again. That's kind of what it was like transitioning from a physical form to spirit form. I arrived at what seemed like a weigh station, a place in between our plane of existence and the next. It was all white—the whitest, brightest light imaginable. I was vibration. I was frequency and complete consciousness. I didn't have a body, and I didn't feel like I needed a body. I could see different variations of the white light. It was amazing. I felt complete release. Off in the distance, I could see these light beings approaching me. I felt that these beings were assigned to me as guides. Their shapes morphed. They would meld together and become one energy, and then, they would come apart into separate figures. There were two of them; one was taller and had a distinct male energy, and the other had a distinct female energy."

Lee continued with her account of what she saw and experienced on the other side. "The two spirit guides spoke to me separately and as one form. I felt no attachment to my previous life; I wanted to stay. The spirit guides told me that I still had free will there, just as I had had in my physical body on earth. I could choose whether to go or to stay. Immediately, I felt like I wanted to stay. I had no doubts about it. They told me that it was my decision. There were things, however, that I should know before I made that decision. I didn't have what some people recall as a "life review;" rather, it was more like a relationship review. Individual people came into my consciousness. I felt the energy of my experience with that person; I felt the vastness of the knowledge, wisdom, and love that was learned from that relationship. It would just like wash over me. I would have the experience, and then, it would dissipate and go away. Then the next one would come, and then the next, and so on. All the energies were very different from each other. The significant ones were with my mother, my husband and my son."

During the time of Lee's NDE, she and her husband were having problems in their marriage. When the relationship review came into her consciousness, however, there was no animosity. She said, "I didn't feel anything towards him but appreciation. There was a sense of love and gratitude, and then it washed away. My son came next, and I felt this feeling of extraordinary love that was beyond measure. The love was pure; it had a higher frequency. I was so grateful for the experience of being this child's mother. Then, like the others before, the feelings washed away. Even after feeling that pure, intense love for my son, I was ready to move on to where I was supposed to go. There was still no attachment. I told the beings that I was ready. They told me that my child would not be able to fulfill his destiny, if I did not return. They explained to me that my son had lost his mother in previous lives. They wanted me to understand how he would feel, if I were to die. It felt like shards of glass ripping through my soul. It was excruciatingly painful. I certainly wouldn't wish that on a child. So, that was it. I told them that I would go back, but that I had some requirements. The first requirement was that I would get to go when my son was an adult and didn't need me anymore. The only other request was that I would not be taken until I had also fulfilled my own journey, and, with that, I came back."

Lee did not feel any kind of judgment from the beings she met. There was no life review and no kind of self judgment. "It was pure bliss!" She exclaimed. "It was pure love and non-attachment. Apparently, I was in a space, before actual transition, that would allow for this return. It seemed that the two light beings had a mission to convince me to stay. They gave me the free will to decide, but they were successful in their mission. When Lee did come back, she was very confused. She explained, "I sat up in bed and thought 'what the hell just happened!' I had been so sick. I knew that I was ready to go. I had no idea how long I was out. As I sat up in bed, I could feel how much better I was. It was a very noticeable difference. I felt 70 to 80 percent better. I felt like there was a residue from the other side left on me. I was looking around at the things in my room with such reverence and appreciation. Everything glowed; everything was beautiful, all the way down to the door hinges. I thought that I needed help because something was not right."

Lee continued, "I called my sister. At that time, she was studying metaphysics. I felt compelled to call her because she knew about things like what had just happened to me. I told her what happened. She let me tell the entire account, and she explained to me that I had just experienced, what she referred to as, an "exit opportunity." She was so exuberant about it that I had to hang up. I was still in this blissful state of being, and her excitement bothered me. After I hung up, I just sat alone in silence for several hours. I then decided to call a friend of mine, who was a very spiritual person. After I told her what happened, she referred me to a spiritual teacher that she knew. It was this lady that told me that I had had a near death experience. She knew because she had had three of them. I told her that something was left on me, a residue of sorts. It felt like every color was brighter, more beautiful, deeper, and more vibrant than before my NDE. It was like everything was alive. She knew exactly what I was saying. She told me that it would last about two weeks and slowly start to dissipate each day. She suggested that I journal every day because I would spend the rest of my life trying to get back to that space. She was right."

Lee's life took another strange turn, for the next morning she woke up with half of her face paralyzed. The virus had activated Bell's Palsy. When she found out she laughed. "I was in such a state of elevated consciousness that I knew I had the answers. I had no fear, when I drove myself to the hospital. I knew that it was a message. I started this constant communication with spirit, God the Creator, the Divine Universe, and things started happening. It was like I was in school while I slept. I would receive information, and I would follow it." She continued to recall the profound change that came over her after her NDE. "Everything that happened prior to my near death experience feels like I read it in a book." She said. "I had no attachment to family and no attachment to people or experiences. I couldn't remember people that I used to work with. I couldn't give you dates that things happened in my life. It all felt like I had just read it all in a book."

At the time of her NDE, Lee was an entrepreneur and running her own business. After her diagnosis of Bell's Palsy, the doctors told her that she might regain control of the section of her face that was paralyzed, but that it would take 6 months to a year. She strongly felt that the diagnosis of Bell's Palsy was a message to change the direction of her life, so she immediately called her business partner. She told her about her experience and then told her that she wanted to close the business. Her business partner was a spiritual person and understood Lee's desire to do something different with her life, and she agreed. "That was the beginning of the change for me." Lee said. "I knew that I had a bigger purpose, and it was not running that business. I knew right away that I had to do something different. I was receiving these messages. I learned to become more aware of what I was getting and sensing. I began to let go of some of my own personal issues. I became a Reiki master and began looking for a place where I could practice Reiki. I had gone to three different places, but none felt right. Then I felt an inner guidance giving me directions, and I mean in a very literal sense. It said, 'turn right here,' and I followed the directions and turned right. Then I heard, 'turn left here.' so I turned left. Then I heard, 'stop and get a cup of coffee,' as I was driving by this little café. I pulled in and got a cup of coffee; it was weird because the café was in an area of one-story office buildings. It was a very nice plaza; it was very clean with lots of greenery. While I was drinking my coffee, I got to talking to the owner of the café. As we were talking, I asked him if he knew if any space was available in the plaza. He said the woman I needed to talk to was just in the café. He told me where to find her, so I went to her office to inquire about a space."

"The next thing I knew, I was negotiating office space with her. I ended up negotiating for more space than I had planned. I asked her to send me the lease. When I got back to my car, I was like 'Oh my God! What am I going to do? I have no money!' I was freaking out. Then I heard the voice in my head again. 'Do you think you have anything to do with this?' It said. Then I was told to write some things down. The things I wrote down were Reiki, classes, retail, how much I was going to charge, and what I was going to need. Then it told me to take what I had written down and talk to my husband about it. I thought to myself that he would never go for this; it was never going to happen. Then "they" told me, 'Go talk to your husband, we'll take care of it. Your mother is going to give you some money.' When I spoke to my husband about it, he told me that it sounded good to him. I then talked to my mother about it, and she gave me $1000.00 to get started. What began as two rooms to do Reiki in grew to a thirteen room six thousand square foot wellness center, which ended up including the very same café that I had gotten coffee in."

Lee's life took a dramatic turn after her near death experience. She feels that her NDE put her on her true path to do what she was meant to do in this life. "It was the most expansive, profound experience that I've ever had." Like so many other NDE survivors, Lee came back with psychic abilities, which she did not have before her NDE. She uses these abilities to help others. She explains, "I have mediumship and intuitive abilities now. I have had some great experiences with those who have transitioned. I think it is really important that the message from the other side comes through." She also became a healer and is a practitioner of Reiki and other modes of energy healing. She has helped thousands learn mindfulness meditation and continues to inspire people as a motivational speaker. Lee's life did indeed go in a new direction after her near death experience. Besides her dedication to helping others, she now feels she has another mission in life. She explains, "I want it to be known that there is no death, it's only a transition. It's simply life after life."

CHAPTER 16

The Paranormal Palace

Nestled in the rolling hills of middle Tennessee, a few miles south of Nashville, sits a beautiful estate owned by Sandy and Sherri Nichols. This large two-story house reflects the southern charm of its owners. The property is idyllic, surrounded by lush forests and the gentle sounds of nature. It is not the kind of house that one would suspect to be haunted, but, ever since it was built in 2005, a wide array of paranormal activity has taken place. These mysterious events have been witnessed by the owners as well as multiple visitors to the property, including this author. So many encounters with the afterlife have happened there that friends of the Nichols' eventually dubbed their home "The Paranormal Palace." The spirits, who visit and reside at The Paranormal Palace, are not evil. They have never showed any malice towards Sandy, Sherri or any of their house guests. Over the years, Sandy and Sherri have learned to live with the restless spirits. Those of us who frequently visit their home know to always expect the unexpected. We are rarely disappointed.

The Paranormal Palace

Sandy related how it all began. "Back in 1992, I began to have a series of dreams. I had the same three dreams on the same three dates for four and a half years. These dreams all had the same geographical location in them. My wife Sherry and I had left Tennessee and moved to Miami, Florida because of her business. When my Mother got sick and was diagnosed with terminal cancer, we returned back to this area to be with her. We began to look for property to build our dream house. On our first day, we came across this property. We loved it so much that, within 15 minutes, we decided to buy it. We bought the first lot and built the first house in the subdivision. It took about a year and half to build our house. About ten months into the building process, I went out there one Sunday afternoon to check on the progress. As I was leaving, I got to the top of the hill that overlooked the valley; I suddenly slammed on my brakes. It hit me, as I was looking at the view, that this was the same geographical valley that I saw in those three recurring dreams."

Sandy recalled that high strangeness began even before the house was complete. He explained that mysterious light anomalies showed up in photos that he took of the house as it was being built, including one that looked like the skull of a horse. Sandy recalled another incident that happened as the house was being constructed. "We were having hardwood floors installed, and the workers had placed these large five-foot tall heaters around to keep the hardwood flooring from warping during the cold snap. I was over at the house late one night checking on things. It was about 10:30, so no one else was there. It had warmed up enough that the workers had turned off all the heaters. I was standing out on the back porch looking around, when I heard footsteps walking around inside the house. It sounded like several people walking around with heavy boots. I, then, heard one of the heaters being dragged across the floor. It sounded like it was dragged about twenty feet. To me, it sounded like a recording of the workers during the day, and I was somehow hearing it. At the time, I did not suspect anything ghostly but knew something very strange was happening."

As the odd occurrences continued, Sandy felt compelled to investigate the history of his land and the surrounding land. He learned that his property had been used for farming for at least one hundred and fifty years. The same family had owned and worked the land during that time. Eventually, he learned that more things had taken place on his property than just farming. Some of which have been related by the ghosts that have been seen by numerous witnesses over the years. "The first ghost was seen by my wife, Sherry, right after we moved in." Sandy stated. "She was sitting in our garage playing with our two black labs, when she saw a guy wearing overalls walk between our cars in the garage." Not long after Sherry's ghostly encounter, Sandy had one of his own. Sandy recalled the incident, "I was sitting in the hot tub alone late one night. Suddenly, to my right, I saw a guy wearing old blue jean overalls. He wasn't by himself; I also saw a woman and a little girl with him. They looked so real. I was thinking to myself, 'where the heck did these people come from?'"

Sandy continued, "I started talking to them. I asked them who they were. They told me their names: George, Barbara, and Libby." Since they appeared to be living people, Sandy thought that they were just odd people who lived somewhere in the area. It was what they told him next that really caught his attention. "They told me that they had been a family of settlers who came here in the late 1700's. They said they were from Europe—the Germany, Austria region. They had come over with a group of people but had settled in this area to be alone. I wasn't sure what to think, so I just let them talk. They told me how much they loved the land around my house. This is where they used to live, until they were run off by Indians. After they moved, they said they were all killed by Indians. As quickly as they appeared, they all just suddenly vanished!" Sandy exclaimed. Since that remarkable encounter, all three of the ghostly figures have been seen at the house, although not all together like they had been on that night. Libby has been seen looking over the upstairs balcony and walking down the hallway towards the master bedroom.

After these two events, Sandy knew that there was more to his land than met the eye. The ghostly encounters continued. Sandy and Sherry soon discovered that there were more restless spirits there than just the forlorn family that appeared to Sandy that night while relaxing in the hot tub. Not only were they seeing and hearing them, but others were as well. Sandy is a paranormal investigator, so he began to use his investigative equipment to contact the other ghosts in the house. He captured various EVPs and mysterious light anomalies on film. He asked this author and other paranormal investigator friends to also join him. I too caught several EVPs; one of which was of a child. This child was a male, so we knew it was not the spirit of Libby. We decided to do a spirit box session to see if we could learn more about the ghosts residing in the home and why they were there. Several of Sandy's friends and fellow paranormal investigators attended the spirit box session. I ran the session. I asked for the little boy in the house to speak to us. We all heard a voice that sounded like a male child. I asked him what his name was. We clearly heard a reply, "Jacob." He told us that he was seven years old. I asked him where his mother and father were, and we heard him say what sounded like, "Bernadette." We assumed that he was telling us his mother's name.

Later, while running the audio file through my software, I slowed down that section. It became clear what Jacob was trying to tell us. Slowed down, it said, "Burned to death." He was telling us that his parents had burned to death. We figured that he might have as well, and that was the reason he crossed over at such a young age. Sandy continued his research of his property and the surrounding area and found out that this was correct. He asked some of the older residents about it. "I found out that there was a barn and an old silo over on the east side of the neighborhood, down in the valley, that had caught on fire and burned down. The remnants of the old silo are still there. There were people who died in the fire. I was told that the accident happened approximately 100 years ago." After learning of the tragedy, we conducted another spirit box session in the hopes of once again contacting little Jacob. This spirit box session was no different than the previous one, and we successfully found Jacob again. He told us that he was happy staying with Sandy and Sherry. We all felt sad for him, as it seemed he did not know why he had not moved on, but we were all glad to know that he was at least content residing in the Paranormal Palace. Sandy told Jacob that he was welcome to stay. In fact, Sandy was kind enough to set up several antique toys and little rocking chairs up in the large unfinished third floor attic of his house for the spirits of Jacob and Libby.

There has been quite a bit of spirit communication and activity up in that third floor attic. When Sandy set up the various toys, tables, and chairs for Libby and Jacob, he marked the floor where the objects were sitting. He did this to see if, at any time, they had been moved. On several occasions, he has observed some of the objects moved out of the marker lines. Not only does it seem that Jacob and Libby visit or reside in the upstairs attic, but other ghosts do also. One of which appears to be the spirit of Libby's mother Barbara. I recall doing an EVP session in that part of the house with Sandy. Sandy asked me, "Why would they want to live up here?" On my digital recorder, I caught an EVP of a woman replying to Sandy's question. She said, "Because we're dead." Several other EVPs have been recorded up there including more from Jacob telling us he liked the toys. On a recent visit to his third floor attic, Sandy heard a woman cry out to him, "Help me." He thought this might be Libby's mother asking for his help, now realizing that they need to move on.

While Sandy was researching the area around his property, he also learned that there was once an old Indian trail that ran alongside his property line and made its way down into an adjacent valley on the other side. During the Civil War, this old Indian trail was also used by soldiers, which could possibly be the reason for another very active ghost that has been seen by several people in the Paranormal Palace. He has appeared as a full body apparition dressed in full uniform and looked to be a ranking officer, either a Colonel or a General. He was also very tall, at least 6'4" or taller. "Mainly, I've seen him in the back part of the house, by the master bedroom and laundry room." Sandy said. Interestingly, that part of the house is the closest to where the old trail was located. One night, Sandy was coming out of the laundry room carrying a basket of clothes. He looked up and came face to face with the Colonel, who was standing in the hallway. The figure of the ghostly soldier then quickly vanished. Naturally, Sandy was startled. Thinking that the ghost might still be around, he spoke to him. "I told him that it is okay for him to stay in our house, but I didn't want him to startle me or anyone else like that again." Since then, the Colonel has made his presence known but in more subtle ways than appearing directly in front of someone.

I had my own sighting of the ghost of the Civil War soldier dubbed the "Colonel" late one night after riding back from a paranormal investigation with Sandy. We pulled into the driveway of The Paranormal Palace around 1AM. I had left my car at Sandy's and rode down to southern Tennessee with him to the location of the investigation. It had been a long drive already, and I still had another thirty-five minutes to drive to my house, so I asked Sandy if I could use the bathroom before driving home. He told me to use the bathroom in the guest house out back because his wife Sherry had already gone to bed, and he did not want to wake her. Sandy escorted me to the guest house, which he also used as his office. He waited outside by the pool, while I used the bathroom. When I came out, he also went in to use the bathroom, and I waited outside. Sherry had left a lamp on in their den that overlooked the pool and guest house, so there was a small amount of light coming from the house. I was looking out across the pool when I saw movement to my left in my peripheral vision. My first thought was that we had awakened Sherry. I turned toward the den expecting to see Sherry. Instead, I saw the Colonel. It looked as though he had walked right through the master bedroom wall. He was walking with a long stride from left to right. He did not look at me; he was looking straight ahead. He took four big steps and then suddenly vanished.

The Colonel has not restricted his movement only to the night time hours. He has also been seen during the day and, as always, as a full body apparition. One afternoon, three maids were upstairs cleaning on the second floor. Two of the maids were busy sweeping and dusting downstairs. The other maid was upstairs vacuuming one of the bedrooms on the second floor, when she looked up and saw the Colonel standing in the doorway of the bedroom watching her. He then turned and walked down the hall. She knew that no other men were in the house besides Sandy, since he always told them if others were in the house. She dropped the vacuum attachment and rushed to look down the hall. The ghostly figure was still walking away from her. He stopped at the end of the hall, looked back at her, and then turned and walked down the stairs toward the first floor. As he did, she saw the bottom part of his body disappear. Frightened by what she saw, she quickly exited the second floor to tell her sisters what had happened. The maid finished the day but was so terrified by the experience that she quit, refusing to ever enter the house again.

Another ghost, regularly seen at the Paranormal Palace, is that of a teenage young man. No one knows who he is or why he is there. He seems to favor the yard area in back of the pool. He has been quite vocal and has communicated through electronic voice phenomena. Through EVP, he has communicated that his name is William. William is the other full body apparition that this author has witnessed at the Paranormal Palace. I was in the foyer of the house sitting with a few other people; I saw someone peek in the small glass window panes of the French doors that lead out to the back porch and pool. The person looked so real that I thought that someone else was coming to visit. "Are you expecting someone else tonight?" I asked Sandy. "No, I'm not. Everyone that was invited is already here." He replied. "Well I just saw a young man looking through the glass on the door." I told the group of friends gathered around. "What did he look like?" Sandy asked. "He was young, maybe 17 or 18 years old." I answered. "That must be William." Sandy concluded. Everyone there had heard the stories about William, and most had heard the EVPs caught out back where he spoke. Immediately, we all jumped up and headed out back. We looked everywhere and found no trace of anyone else at Sandy's house. It seemed that the gathering of people that night had indeed stirred up William's curiosity.

Sandy has also had a close encounter with William. Knowing that the ghost of William is most often seen and recorded in the back yard area, Sandy decided to try and catch William on film. "It was late one night, about 2AM, and I got this idea to go out behind the pool where William favors to snap a few pictures. I knew it was a long shot, but I thought I'd try and capture him on film. I walked out the back-pool gate about fifteen feet into the yard and began taking a few pictures, pointing the camera in different areas of the backyard as I did. After several minutes of taking photos, I decided that I wasn't going to catch anything. As I was lowering the camera, I accidently took one last picture. In the light from the camera flash, there stood William, right next to me. He was wearing a jacket with a white shirt. The collar on his shirt stood straight up. His clothing looked dated. He looked like he had just come from church or was dressed for some type of special function." To this day, no one knows who William is or why he is at the Paranormal Palace.

Sandy recalled another unexplainable incident that happened to him, which has him believing that there may be some type of dimensional overlap happening on the grounds of their home. Given the wide array of paranormal events that take place on the property, the idea of a dimensional overlap or portal is a real possibility. "I had lain down out in my office in the guest house to take a brief nap. I was sleeping, when I was awakened by someone knocking on the door. No one was home except Sherry and me, and we always communicated by intercom, so it was very unusual for anyone to be knocking on the door of my office." Sandy continued, "I went to the door, and no one was there. Then I heard someone making a moaning sound. I had heard sounds around my office on other occasions. One night I was in my office, and my wife was already asleep in the house. Suddenly, I heard a man and several women talking. The man was doing most of the talking. It sounded like they were in the attic storage area of the pool house right above me. Thinking that someone was on the property and was going to try and rob us, I hurried into the house to wake my wife Sherry. I had her sit out by the pool house with her gun. I grabbed my gun and our two dogs and went around to the back of the pool house where the entrance to the attic was. It was winter, and there was a heavy frost on the ground. When I went out the back gate, I noticed that there were no footprints anywhere, but I was still hearing people talking. I wasn't sure what was happening. I thought that, if they weren't planning on breaking in, maybe they were homeless and had somehow gotten to our house and climbed up in the attic to keep warm. When I got around to the entrance of the attic, I pulled down the stairs and climbed up there. I found nothing; no one was up there. The dogs also were quiet, so I knew that there was no one else around. I apologized to Sherry, and she went back to the main house and went back to bed."

Sandy chalked it all up to another night of high strangeness at his house and went back into his office in the pool house. No sooner had he returned when he began to hear the voices again. "This time it was the women who were doing most of the talking. I remained very quiet. I tried to listen closely to their conversation. I wanted to know what they were talking about. Then I heard the guy playing guitar!" Sandy exclaimed. "I could hear the woman telling him how good he was. There were three different female voices giving him compliments on his guitar playing. This went on for close to fifteen minutes. I didn't know what to do to make them stop. It was like I was listening to people in another dimension at a party or something. I started to get a bit aggravated by the whole thing. I had already woken Sherry once, and I didn't want to wake her up again, so I decided to sleep in my office. How was I going to get any sleep with all this noise above me? It was now past 1AM, and I had to get up early the next morning. I decided to speak to them in the hopes that they could hear me. I yelled out, 'Hey! I'm going to be going to bed here in a few minutes. Do you think you could hold off the music?' Suddenly, everything went quiet; there were no more voices or music."

There could be a myriad of reasons as to why Sandy and Sherry's beautiful home and the surrounding land is engulfed in spirit activity, energy anomalies, and dimensional high strangeness. One of the most prevalent reasons would be the location. As previously mentioned, the house sits very near an old trail that was used by Confederate soldiers during the Civil War. During the time that the Union soldiers had control of nearby Nashville, there was an estimated three thousand Confederate guerrilla soldiers roaming the area around the house. The trail was used by the Confederates because it was an already established trail, having been used by the Native Americans in the area.

Due to all the balls of light and high rate of paranormal activity at the Paranormal Palace, I had always felt that there must be some type of dimensional portal there, possibly associated and brought on by ley lines. Many mysterious places around the earth are noted for having these naturally occurring ley lines running through them. Ley lines are straight lines of increased levels of positive electromagnetic energy. One night during a gathering of friends at the house, I mentioned to Lamar Hamilton, a very well-known psychic and friend, my theory about that. The idea resonated with him, and he immediately picked up on it psychically. He said that he agreed. He then began to point them out. We decided to go out back, and Lamar began to use markers to tell me where he felt the ley lines were. He pointed to the kitchen fireplace and said that one went right through the house there. He then pointed to a tree along the edge of the old trail and said that it continued that way. I had some ghost hunting equipment in my car. I told Lamar to wait right there, while I went to check out my equipment. I do not usually keep dowsing rods with my equipment, but I just happened to have some with me. I grabbed a couple of sets of them and returned to where Lamar was. I wanted to use the dowsing rods since it is believed that, when properly used, they can pinpoint ley lines.

By this time, others at the gathering had joined us. We explained what Lamar was sensing, and we were going to use the dowsing rods to validate what he was sensing. A couple of people from the group began to use them, and, sure enough, the rods reacted to the exact area where Lamar had identified a ley line. We then proceeded to walk out to the tree, along the edge of the woods by the old trial and followed the ley line. The dowsing rods were still following it. As we neared the tree, Lamar said that he sensed another ley line. This one was crossing the first one and headed out in a different direction. When we arrived at the point where the ley lines crossed, the dowsing rods began to spin like helicopter blades! It did not matter who held them, they would spin. As we followed the second ley line, Lamar began to pick up more about the land. He felt that the area, surrounding Sandy's house, was a sacred area to the local Native Americans, who had once inhabited the land. He said he saw ceremonial processions and events happening there. It all began to make sense. Somehow, many of the ancients across the globe had picked areas with strong ley lines for sacred rituals. Perhaps, the same thing happened on the land at the Paranormal Palace.

After that night, Sandy began to explore further into the woods behind his house. He discovered a strange flat rock formation with matching surrounding rocks that looked very much like it was some kind of meeting place or even an alter. He then found two stones that looked like large footprints. In 2017, Sandy was walking along the tree line in his backyard, when he felt strongly compelled to start digging. It did not make sense to him, but he could not shake the feeling. So, he got a shovel and started digging. Eventually, he found what appeared to be a man-made stone path. All of his mysterious finds give credence to the possibility that the land was indeed special and was used as a sacred site by the Native Americans. Did these ancient ceremonies open up dimensional portals to the other side? Do the countless lost souls that come and go at the Paranormal Palace simply use the strong energy from the ley lines to manifest and communicate to Sandy, Sherry and the many visitors who have witnessed and encountered them there? Whatever the reason, one thing is for sure—afterlife encounters are the norm rather than the exception at the Paranormal Palace.

Chapter 17

In The Presence Of God

Life has its ups and downs, for all of us. We do our best to maneuver through its many twists and turns. For Debra Jayne East, life took a serious turn for the worse, when she was 49 years old. Her marriage of 18 years had just ended, leaving her a single Mom of two young boys. As she approached her birthday that year, she received more bad news. "My 50th birthday was coming in March, and I can say that I wasn't looking forward to it." Debra said. "Then I found out that I needed a total knee arthroplasty, which is a surgical procedure in which parts of the knee joint are replaced with artificial parts. Three years earlier, the highway pavement had not been kind to me, when I was thrown by a Belgium workhorse named Lucy. Lucy was one of several horses we had raised on our farm. I went through almost three months of physical therapy after the accident. I also had the meniscus repaired in my knee, but it did not help."

Debra continued, "The surgery was scheduled right before my birthday. I was to be there for a few days and was not going to be released until the day after my birthday. So, I would hit the big five-o milestone while in the hospital. I had a female surgeon named Dr. Hansen, who assured me that I would be fine. I had had two other surgeries before, and I knew what to expect; it was no big deal to me." Debra's daughter, Misty, and her husband accompanied her to the hospital the day of the surgery. Debra had sent her two sons to school that day and had arranged for Misty to pick them up after school. She was confident that this would be a routine surgery. As fate would have it, the surgery turned out to be anything but routine. Unbeknownst to the doctors at the time, Debra had a heart condition called "atrial fibrillation," which is a dangerous heart malfunction that causes the heart to go into an abnormal rhythm, characterized by rapid and irregular beating. Soon after the surgery began, Debra went into full cardiac arrest.

"The last thing I consciously remembered was the IV drip in my arm, as I dissolved into nothingness." Debra recalled. Then something strange happened to Debra. Even though she was under anesthesia, she could hear sounds in the room. "The sounds came first; they were frantic sounds from the nurses. I could hear my heartbeat amplified really loud on the monitors. There seemed to be a lot of doctors and nurses rustling around the room. I could hear the machines starting to make beeping sounds like some kind of alert signal. 'Her heart rate is up over 200 BPM!' A nurse yelled out." At this point in time, it seemed like Debra was caught between our world and the next, but then the sounds slowly faded out. "Suddenly, I realized that I was watching the whole ordeal above my body. My eyes were closed on my body, but I could see everything going on in the room. Very quickly, I began to float up. I was standing upright, and I floated up to the top of the doorway. I was looking in front of me. It took me awhile to adjust to what was happening because it didn't make any sense to me. I was in a kind of suspended state with no physical body. I seemed to be moving within a white glowing mist. I had no pain. I didn't feel any fear. Actually, I felt disassociated from all of it. I was just observing."

Misty and her husband were in a waiting room one floor below the operating room. As Debra was floating above the door of the operating room, she saw a nurse run out the door and down the hall. "I knew that the nurse wasn't going to get another doctor or more nurses. I had an inner knowing that the nurse was going to talk to my daughter, and I knew what she was going to tell her. Somehow, I could see down through the floors of the hospital into the waiting room where my daughter was. It was like having x-ray vision. I saw the same nurse go into the waiting room where my daughter and son-in-law were. I didn't hear the nurse say any words. It was more like I was watching a silent movie. I saw the nurse shaking her head as she was talking. I saw my daughter start to cry, as she began praying for me. Her head was bowed, and her shoulders shook softly. I couldn't hear my daughter's prayers, but I knew that she was praying for me."

It was at that point that things began to change for Debra, and a new realization set in. She explained, "Right after I saw my daughter praying me, my surroundings began to change. Everything around me faded out. I knew that I was no longer in the physical world. A very bright white mist or haze enveloped me. It looked like clouds, but it wasn't clouds. I knew that I had died. The next thing I saw were, what I perceived as, Angelic beings. I could hear their voices reverberating all around. I couldn't quite make out their faces, but they all looked very similar. They were tall and wore long white robes. There were rows and rows of them. They were lined up off in the distance and stopped at, what I felt was, God's throne." It was then that Debra's experience got even more profound. "I felt the presence of God!" Debra exclaimed. "It was so strong and powerful. If I had had a body, I would have fallen to my knees. I felt greatly humbled and too shy to look towards him. I describe God as a male, but there wasn't any kind of physical body that I saw. It was a presence. It's difficult to describe just how big God felt. He filled the space I was in and everything else around it. It was like God was the universe."

Somewhere deep inside her heart, Debra felt that it was not her time to leave her earthbound physical body. She gathered up her nerve to speak to God. She recalled her words, "In my disembodied state, I could hear my thoughts out loud. 'God'…. I begged. 'Would you let me stay a little while longer?' 'I want to help people.' I explained. "God granted my request. Everything faded at that instant. I woke up 24 hours later in the ICU of the hospital, where I remained for the next eight days. I did not remember my name without looking at my ID bracelet, but I remembered speaking to my creator when my heart had stopped beating. I remembered everything that had happened during my near death experience. I asked my daughter if she began to pray for me after the nurse came into the waiting the room. She told me the sequence of events, and it was exactly what I had seen while looking through the floors of the hospital. As I recovered, I felt differently: physically, spiritually and mentally. I knew that I would never be the same again. My life had forever been changed by my visit to the other side."

There were new challenges awaiting Debra on her road to recovery. After her surgery, she became very depressed. This is common for heart patients. It goes along with the condition. On top of that, she was still coping with her divorce and the heavy burden of being a single mother. It was all too much for her. Debra's depression was severe. So much so that she became suicidal. Debra recounted the mysterious event that happened next. "I had made up my mind that I was going to kill myself. I planned on driving my car over a cliff. That day I took my two sons over to my daughter's house. I pulled into her driveway and stopped. My boys got out and ran into her house. I was just going to tell my daughter that I was going for a drive. I began to cry. With tears running down my face, I opened the car door and stood beside my car. For some reason I felt compelled to reach my hand into the grass beside my car. I was crying so much that I couldn't see much of anything. As my hand went through the grass, I touched upon a small object and pulled it out of the grass. It was a quartz crystal in the shape of a crooked heart. Then I heard a voice so loud and clear that I looked around to see if someone had pulled in behind me. The voice said, 'Even though your heart is broken and even though you feel like you can never love again, you still have a heart, and you can still love.' Then I looked at the heart shaped stone I was holding in my hand. It had a big crack in it, and it was all beat up and I thought, 'Wow! I'm not really broken. My heart is still a heart. I can still love again.' That event saved my life."

That incident not only saved Debra's life; it changed it too. "All of a sudden my life became normal. I had always had a dream of writing a book, so I decided to go ahead and write it. I thought 'all I have to do is write the book, and I knew that it would be published.' Three months later, I finished the book. Four months after that, I found a publisher, and it was published. It's called *Radiance, Love After Death,* and it is about the experience of a woman getting killed in a car accident and waking up on the other side. It went on to be a bestselling book on Amazon." Even stranger is the fact that Debra did not have any writing experience at all. She didn't even know how to use the Microsoft Word software she needed to write her book. She had to learn it, as she wrote her book. The basic premise of the story seemed to parallel her recent life events. She stated that it just unfolded as she wrote. Thankfully she didn't drive over a cliff that day and kill herself. Once again divine intervention altered her life and set her off in the direction she was supposed to go in.

Another thing that changed in Debra was her interest in life on other planets and in all things paranormal in general. That interest grew so strong that she started her own radio show about those subjects, which she still hosts to this day. Some of the guests on her radio show were people who claimed to have been abducted by aliens. From her numerous interviews and discussions with them, she discovered something very odd. "There are so many alien abductees who have had near death experiences." Debra revealed. One of the people she met became a mentor and teacher to Debra. She explained, "This particular woman had a terrible accident. She had died and was resuscitated several times as the paramedics were frantically trying to save her life. Like so many others who've had a DNE, she came back with psychic abilities. Her abilities are the strongest I've ever seen in any human being. She has coached me and helped me to have clearer vision to deal with the energies I pick up from people, both positive and negative. Through her coaching, I've been able to steer away from negative people and those who wish to harm me. Moreover, I've learned to use my ability to read and feel energy to help and guide others." Much of what Debra learned about the strange correlation between alien abductees and those who experienced an NDE, this author has learned as well. Almost every alien abductee has come back with some sort of psychic ability, as have people who have had a near death experience. If they did not have psychic abilities before the incident, they did afterwards. If they did exhibit some psychic awareness before, it was greatly enhanced once they returned. Another striking similarity is how both groups' view of the world and religion change after these profound events. They all become more altruistic, many becoming strong advocates for humanity, the environment, and animals.

Debra sought to learn more about what she had experienced. "I wanted to know how the body is different after you die." She explained. "At first, I came up with DMT, Dimethyltryptamine is an intense, naturally occurring psychedelic that's also found endogenously in the human body and is stored in the pineal gland. When you die, it is released into the body. Perhaps, that has something to do with it. Once you're activated, so to speak, you can't really turn that off again. I read a book about DMT, which is also referred to as the, "The Spirit Molecule." In the book, the author presented a theory that the purpose of DMT in the human body was to help people transition from a living state of existence to a non-living state; whatever that was. Perhaps, the enhanced psychic abilities happen in those who have entered into that non-living state, even if only temporarily, because of that DMT release and pineal gland activation. No one really knows for sure, but it's an intriguing theory none the less."

Debra has visited the other side and was humbled by the presence of the All of Everything. She knows what a blessing that was and will be forever grateful for being giving a second chance at this life. She is keeping her promise of helping people that she made that day to the Creator. Debra continues on her quest for answers to life's greatest mystery. She leaves us with these final thoughts on it, "We all change from that kind of event. It is something that is beyond human understanding. I am still learning. Every day is a gift, but death does not bother me anymore."

CHAPTER 18

The End Is Not The End

Fear. No matter where we live in the world or what our cultural or belief systems are, most humans are controlled by fear. These beliefs can be so ingrained in our psyche that we do not even realize how much they control us. One of the greatest fears we have is the fear of death. It is the uncertainty of death that ignites our fear; we do not know when or how it will happen. We feel unsettled when we contemplate what really happens after we take our last breath. Sure, religion teaches us that, if we have lived a good life, our souls end up in heaven, but even that elicits some degree of fear, no matter how strong one's faith is. What if you did not live a good enough life? Will you be judged? Will you be cast into Hell to burn for all eternity? Some believe that there is nothing on the other side; we simply just stop being. Perhaps, a line from the Kenny Chesney song, "Everybody Wants to Go to Heaven," says it best. In it, the lyric goes, "Everybody wants to go to Heaven, but nobody wants to go now." Truer words have never been written. That small flame of the fear of death burns in all of us regardless of who we are or what our beliefs are. This book was written to help ease or, perhaps, even erase those long held fears.

There are those who have learned not to fear death because they have done it and have come back to tell us what it is like. These are the individuals who have had a near death experience. They are the exception, and, as we learned from the accounts in this book, they no longer fear death. This was unanimous among the contributors who have gone through an NDE. In fact, they described the death transition as an encompassing feeling of profound bliss and an unconditional love so intense that many had trouble finding the proper words to really explain just how wonderful it was. They also described feeling a complete detachment from the material world. Each of them alluded to life altering changes after the experience. Some found their true path as a result of the experience. Most have changed their religious views and seek inclusivity rather than strict dogmatism. They now consider themselves as deeply spiritual and not religious, per se. It was interesting that none of them saw or experienced anything that they perceived as Hell. As mentioned earlier in this book, most developed some sort of psychic ability or enhanced psychic awareness as a result of their NDE. All the people interviewed for this book, who had a near death experience, returned to the world of the living because they still had work to do here. Every single one of them looks forward to someday returning to that ethereal state just beyond the physical body.

It is quite evident that we all have what we call a "soul" and that it/we continue on after death of the physical body. After all, we are made up of energy, and the law of conservation of energy states that energy cannot be created nor destroyed, only transferred from one form to another. That is the death process. We simply transfer from one form (our physical earth-bound body) to another (our non-physical self), which is no longer restrained to this dimension. Sometimes there are those who, for various reasons, do not make the full transition to where they are supposed to go. They end up getting trapped in this plane of existence. They become what we refer to as a "ghost." The ghosts, written about in this book, did not seem particularly frightening to the people who encountered them. Some seemed to be confused and not fully aware that they had died. Others stayed because they wanted to remain; they were not ready to let go of this material world. Perhaps, they were tied to someone or someplace still on earth. Most were not trying to scare the living but rather trying to make contact in whatever way possible. They wanted acknowledgment of their existence, or they wanted someone to help them cross over to their final place of rest. Not every so called "haunting" is evil or demonic, as Hollywood would like us to believe. It should be noted than none of the NDE contributors saw anything dark, evil, or demonic on the other side. Once again, it is that emotion of fear that comes into play when one thinks about the reality of ghosts. We are programmed from an early age to fear ghosts, or we are taught that they do not exist at all. This makes it even more frightening if or when one does encounter a ghost. It is our hope that people will let go of the fear of ghosts and instead look at them with compassion and empathy. Some want to be left alone and are happy to be here, but most are lost, confused, and scared. They need us to help them.

Further proof that our soul carries on came from the numerous incredible accounts of those who had received messages from loved ones who had passed. The contact from their departed friends and relatives came in many different forms and signs including: seeing the spirit, hearing their voice, seeing physical objects appear, and experiencing synchronistic events connected to the spirit. Often these messages were simply the spirits letting the living know that they are okay and happy where they are. It is their way of saying that they are still with them, that there is no real death. Other times, the deceased loved one would give warnings, which sometimes saved lives. It seems that transitioning through the veil does not stop us from doing what we can to protect and guide those we love in the realm of the living. Everyone that experienced an afterlife encounter of this kind was not frightened by the experience but rather found great comfort in it. All felt deep gratitude and blessed that it had happened to them.

It is imperative to have an open mind about the afterlife as there is much to learn from those who have had a near death experience, a ghost sighting, or communication from a spirit. We learned from the stories in this book that these types of experiences happen to people from all walks of life regardless of gender, race, culture, or religious beliefs. These encounters change people's life in a positive way. The spirits, of those who have gone on before us, have much to teach us, if we are willing to listen. They want us to know that consciousness continues on after death. We detach from the things in our material world when we cross over, so the love for those things is meaningless and, in fact, could keep us from progressing in our soul journey. They want us to know that love transcends death and is a bond that cannot be broken. From these accounts, we have learned that the fear of death is an unfounded one. There is nothing to fear about death because, in essence, there is no real death. It is merely energy transitioning from one form to another. It is indeed the afterlife—a continuation of life and a new beginning. The end is not the end....

Works Cited List

www.octagonhall.com

www.kyhistory.com

Story, Justin. Bowling Green Daily News, June 8, 2013 Issue

Story, Justin. Bowling Green Daily News, November 14, 2012 Issue

Raudive, Konstantin. Breakthrough: An Amazing Experiment in Electronic Communication With The Dead. Taplinger Publishing, (1971)

Fontana, David. Is There An Afterlife: A Comprehensive Review of the Evidence. Hants, UK: O Books (2005)

Cardosa, Anabela. "ITC Voices: Contact With Another Reality?" (HTML) Paper. (2003)

Swartz, Tim R. The Lost Journals of Nikola Tesla: Time Travel, Alternative Energy and the Secret of Nazi Flying Saucers. Inner Light/Conspiracy Journal.com, February 8, 2012

Raynes, Brent. AP Magazine, January, 2011 Issue

Printed in Great Britain
by Amazon

45307919R00084